Anxiety Unmasked During the COVID-19 Pandemic

A Global Mental Health Concern

Charletta Dennis, M.D., CCHP

© Copyright 2022 - All rights reserved.

The content contained within this book may not be reproduced, duplicated or transmitted without direct written permission from the author or the publisher.

Under no circumstances will any blame or legal responsibility be held against the publisher, or author, for any damages, reparation, or monetary loss due to the information contained within this book, either directly or indirectly.

Legal Notice:

This book is copyright protected. It is only for personal use. You cannot amend, distribute, sell, use, quote or paraphrase any part, or the content within this book, without the consent of the author or publisher.

Disclaimer Notice:

Please note the information contained within this document is for educational and entertainment purposes only. All effort has been executed to present accurate, up to date, reliable, complete information. No warranties of any kind are declared or implied. Readers acknowledge that the author is not engaged in the rendering of legal, financial, medical or professional advice. The content within this book has been derived from various sources. Please consult a licensed professional before attempting any techniques outlined in this book.

By reading this document, the reader agrees that under no circumstances is the author responsible for any losses, direct or indirect, that are incurred as a result of the use of the information contained within this document, including, but not limited to, errors, omissions, or inaccuracies.

Table of Contents

INTRODUCTION 1
    THE AUTHOR 2
CHAPTER 1: WHAT IS ANXIETY? 3
    FORMS OF ANXIETY 4
        Generalized Anxiety Disorder 4
        Panic Disorder 6
        Social Anxiety Disorder 7
        Phobia-Related Disorders 8
        Pandemic Anxiety 10
    ANXIETY TRIGGERS 11
        Stress 11
        Medication 12
        Negative Thoughts 12
        Health Issues 13
        Conflict 14
        Lifestyle Habits 14
        Personal Triggers 16
        Self-Neglect 16
    YOU AND ANXIETY 18
        Mental Health 18
        Memory Loss 18
        Weight Gain 19
        Alcohol and Drug Abuse 19
CHAPTER 2: THE DAMAGE DONE 21
    COVID-19 AND EMPLOYMENT 21
    COVID-19 AND EDUCATION 23
    COVID-19 AND HEALTHCARE 25
    COVID-19 AND SOCIAL INTERACTIONS 26
    COVID-19 AND STIGMATIZATION 27

THE IMPACT OF COVID-19 ON ANXIETY 28
    Grief 28
    Denial 30
    Despair 31
    Relationship Tension 32
    Life Hardships 33

CHAPTER 3: WAYS TO COPE 35

SELF-CARE 35
    Physical Self-Care 36
    Emotional Self-Care 42
    Social Self-Care 46
    Mental and Spiritual Self-Care 53
    Self-Care Plan Strategies 56

CHAPTER 4: DEALING WITH ANXIETY 59

AVOIDING TRIGGERS 59
    Frequent COVID-19 Updates 60
    Misinformation 60
    Official Guidelines 61
    Vaccination 62
    Avoiding the Talk 62
    Refreshing Yourself 63
ADDRESSING STIGMATIZATION 63
    Tips to Combat Stigma 64
PROFESSIONAL HELP 66
    Primary Care Physician 68
    Psychologist 69
    Psychiatric Nurse Practitioners and Physician Assistants ... 69
    Psychiatrist 69
    When to See a Doctor 70
    Preparing to See a Doctor 72
THERAPY 75
    Types of Therapy for Anxiety 76
    Psychoanalytic Therapy 79
    Interpersonal Therapy 80

CHAPTER 5: TREATMENT OPTIONS 83
- Selective Serotonin Reuptake Inhibitors 83
- Serotonin-Norepinephrine Reuptake Inhibitors 85
- Benzodiazepines 87
- Buspirone 89
- Beta Blockers 90
- Hydroxyzine 93

CHAPTER 6: MOVING ON 95
- Dealing with Loss 95
  - *Stages of Grief* 96
- Peace and Happiness 105
  - *Find Your Joy* 108

CONCLUSION 111

REFERENCES 113

Introduction

Several people have suffered the effects of the COVID-19 pandemic, and living without any certain news about it is unsettling. *Anxiety Unmasked During the Pandemic* gives you a starting point to help work your way toward leading a happy and positive life even with all the uncertainty that is in the air.

This guide targets individuals with anxiety challenges and provides practical strategies to deal with anxiety during the pandemic. If you are living with anxiety during this difficult time, this guide will help you overcome it by giving you a sound understanding of its symptoms and simple ways to approach the situation based on how you feel. Always remember that you are not alone. Understand that you can seek treatment and learn to cope once you realize that there is hope for you.

The Author

Charletta Dennis, M.D., CCHP, is a diplomate in Psychiatry and Forensic Psychiatry and a certified consulting forensic examiner licensed to practice in Michigan, Wisconsin, Arkansas, Louisiana, North Carolina, Nevada, Kentucky, Virginia, Delaware and California. She has testified as an Expert Witness in both Criminal and Civil proceedings throughout the state of Michigan. She has been featured as an expert on several episodes of the popular true crime TV show For My Man. Dr. Dennis received her medical degree from Wayne State University School of Medicine and completed her residency in Psychiatry at Wayne State University/Henry Ford Health System. She completed her Forensic Psychiatry Fellowship training at the University of Michigan and the Center for Forensic Psychiatry. She is certified by the American Board of Psychiatry and Neurology in Psychiatry and Forensic Psychiatry. She is also certified in Correctional Health Care by the National Commission of Correctional Health Care. She was the Director of Psychiatry for Michigan's Wayne County Jail prior to her promotion to Executive State Psychiatric Director at Grand Prairie/Wellpath overseeing psychiatric care for the Michigan Department of Corrections. She is currently the Chief Medical Officer of Forensic Psychiatric Services, PLLC.

Chapter 1:

What is Anxiety?

Pandemic anxiety is a threat to your mental well-being during and after times of crisis. It stems from a combination of unstable emotions that result from constant worry and fear of occurrences beyond our control. Before we delve into such a complex yet delicate issue, it is essential that you understand anxiety in general and master the basic idea of how much damage uncontrolled anxiety impacts on your mental health. You can then work toward a solution that works best for your situation.

Anxiety can warn us of impending threats and assist us in planning and paying attention. The occasional worry prompts us to take safety measures, and the fear triggers us to seek refuge or fight back in response to certain situations. As a natural response to stress, fears and worries are essential to what makes us human. Still, anxiety becomes a problem when one loses control of the worrying to an extent so intense the fears interfere with daily activities. Excessive fears that constantly interrupt one's usual way of life are known as anxiety disorders. These do not fade away with time, and they can worsen over time unless one deals with them.

Forms of Anxiety

Anxiety disorders are a common mental illness, afflicting about one-third of all adults at some point in their lives (Muskin, 2021). Each form of anxiety disorder manifests differently in each separate individual due to various factors that we will soon discuss.

It is essential to understand that mental healthcare professionals use a set of standard guidelines to diagnose patients with mental health problems, and these guidelines are found in the *Diagnostic and Statistical Manual of Mental Disorders*, a tool published by the American Psychiatric Association, and is currently in its fifth version. For this book, however, we will keep all definitions and explanations simple.

Generalized Anxiety Disorder

Sometimes people with anxiety just worry. In generalized anxiety disorder, affected individuals tend to stress over common issues and activities such as household chores, prices of goods, vehicle maintenance, and many other simple matters. What sets this kind of worry with the occasional concern about costs of goods and cleaning the house is that someone who suffers from generalized anxiety disorder (GAD) can't stop obsessing over their fears. GAD is characterized by persistent and uncontrollable worry that disrupts daily activities. People with GAD experience physical symptoms such as fatigue and mental disturbances such as lack of concentration.

When you have generalized anxiety disorder, you are continuously concerned about anything that could go wrong. You may stress over something negative you think might happen to your loved ones, and as you overthink it, you may realize you can't do much to guarantee their safety, and that sense of helplessness can drive you insane. As the name suggests, if you have GAD, you just worry in general.

As generalized as it is, one requires a professional to confirm GAD as their diagnosis. It can be difficult for individuals to bring themselves up to mental healthcare providers because people can easily shrug the symptoms away and assume it's the usual concern everyone experiences. Below are some of the signs that signal generalized anxiety disorder.

- restlessness
- concentration difficulties
- fatigue
- unexplained body pains
- stomachaches
- irritability
- unhealthy sleep habits
- headaches

Panic Disorder

People with panic attacks may mistakenly feel as though they are having a heart attack or another life-threatening illness due to the severity of the symptoms. Panic attacks can be predicted, such as one's reaction to an object they are afraid of, or they can occur out of nowhere. With sudden attacks that manifest out of the blue, one can go from a house party to a hospital emergency room within a short period, despite no apparent signs of impending danger.

Recurrent panic attacks and an overpowering combination of physical and psychological anguish are the most prominent signs that differentiate panic disorder from other anxiety challenges. Many of the following symptoms occur in tandem during a panic attack:

- dizziness
- pounding heartbeat
- hot flashes or chills
- sweating
- chest pains
- trembling or shaking
- abdominal pains or nausea
- shortness of breath
- numbness or tingling

- fainting

Social Anxiety Disorder

We all understand being nervous when preparing for a job interview and getting sweaty hands before walking onto a stage to address many people. That is normal because, in the end, most of us get through and would have performed just fine. When it comes to people with uncontrolled social anxiety disorders, surviving social situations is a dream. These individuals experience substantial anxiety in social settings and are afraid of being rejected, embarrassed, or looked down on. They strive to avoid circumstances that make them anxious and uncomfortable. Living with social anxiety disorder is more complicated and difficult than it may sound because we are talking about fear or anxiety that significantly interferes with daily functioning and lasts at least six months.

Because everyone is unique and interprets situations in their own way, each individual with social anxiety disorder experiences it in distinct ways. However, they usually have challenges with some, not necessarily all, of the following situations:

- speaking in public
- talking to strangers
- going to school or work
- attending parties
- making eye contact

- initiating conversations
- entering occupied rooms
- dating
- using public restrooms
- eating in public

When exposed to such situations, people with social anxiety disorder may exhibit physical symptoms that include:

- blushing
- rapid heartbeat
- breathlessness
- muscle tension
- sweating
- nausea
- feeling as though they are out of themselves
- dizziness and lightheadedness

Phobia-Related Disorders

A phobia is a strong dislike or fear of a specific place, object, or situation. Unlike anxiety disorders in general, phobias are usually associated with something specific.

Depending on the particular aversion in question and how badly the person dreads the situation, the effects of their phobia range from irritating to profoundly crippling. While it is understandable to feel uncomfortable in some cases, the dread or fear that people with phobias experience is disproportional to the actual risk the object or situation in question may pose. People with phobias know that their anxiety or dread is out of proportion or that the thing or situation in question may not be inherently dangerous. Still, they can't stop themselves from fearing or hating that situation.

When we hate something, or it gives us chills, it is only natural that we try by all means possible to avoid being close to it or situations that may trigger the fear. If one is scared of spiders, they will avoid every crack and crevice where spiders are most likely lurking. Well, that may be understandable, but what if the fear is directly linked to something of significant importance, such as a job in construction when one is scared of heights, or aviophobia, the fear of flying when one has to make frequent business or work-related trips by air? We will soon discuss how these problems impact our lives if left uncontrolled, but first, let's take a peek into the symptoms of phobias. These include, but are not limited to:

- pounding heartbeat
- dry mouth
- shortness of breath
- trembling or shaking
- profuse sweating

- inability to speak, rapid or altered speech
- choking
- upset stomach
- chest pain
- nausea
- feeling as though they are on the brink of death
- elevated blood pressure

Pandemic Anxiety

Disease outbreaks hinder progress in the affected areas and trigger mental unrest in both affected and unaffected populations. The COVID-19 pandemic is an excellent example that has caused disruptions in several areas of various people's lives. Misleading information and rumors can make you feel out of control and unsure of what to do. You may worry about getting sick, how long the pandemic will last, whether your employment will be affected, and how to move forward. You may experience tension, despair, and anxiety due to the uncertainties that pandemics create. We will soon discuss more about anxiety during the COVID-19 pandemic.

Anxiety Triggers

Knowing anxiety triggers help control your anxiety, enabling you to improve your overall well-being. As with the symptoms of anxiety disorders we previously discussed, different individuals have different objects and settings that trigger their anxiety switches. These triggers are innumerable, so we cannot discuss them all, but in this section, we will discuss a few common ones. Most other motivations stem from common triggers, so understanding the major ones will help you identify minor triggers without challenges.

Stress

At one point or another, each individual experiences stressful moments. Stress is an unavoidable aspect of life, but worse, it also triggers anxiety. Everyday stressors, such as traffic delays or missing a necessary appointment, can induce stress in anyone. Long-term stress, on the other hand, can lead to long-term anxiety, worsen symptoms, and other health issues. Stress can also lead to bad lifestyle habits such as missing meals, drinking too much alcohol, and sleeping too little, all of which can cause or exacerbate anxiety.

Although experiencing excessive stress toward tests and interviews characterizes a form of performance anxiety with a name of its own, it triggers other types of anxiety in individuals undergoing the pressure of sitting tests. Test anxiety is sometimes due to one's unpreparedness and lack of study, but it can also happen due to one's dread of failure. When one so intensely wants to pass a test that they can't stay calm, it may trigger different thoughts, eventually getting them a ticket to anxiety.

Controlling stress is incredibly tough, which makes controlling the anxiety that results even more challenging. While there are numerous methods for reducing stress, choosing one that works best for you and your circumstances is critical.

Medication

Certain drugs contain active chemicals that may cause you to feel uneasy, triggering unwanted thoughts and feelings. Both prescription and over-the-counter medicines can have this effect on an individual; it just varies from person to person. Some medications that can trigger anxiety include drugs for weight management, birth control, and even some cough medications.

Negative Thoughts

Several people living with anxiety problems cannot do without *what ifs*. It's almost as if their brain feeds on the countless questions about endless possibilities. Still, in reality, their insurmountable fear of uncertainties and the endless questions feed on their brain, making them overthink everything they know.

People who have challenges controlling their thoughts may find themselves wondering about foul and disturbing occurrences such as them getting a serious medical diagnosis, getting involved in a fatal accident, failing an important interview, and many other ideas. They don't just think about themselves; they may also speculate about something bad happening to their loved ones and other people around them.

When we look deeper into it, how can one not feel anxious if they are constantly exploring negative possibilities?

With negative thinking, when you get angry or frustrated, the things you say to yourself can make you feel even more anxious. How you think plays a significant role in regulating anxiety, but if you are part of *Team What Ifs*, you might not be able just to stop one day. Surviving disturbing thoughts is a process and takes determination.

Health Issues

An upsetting or difficult health diagnosis, such as dementia, cancer, or other chronic illnesses, can provoke or exacerbate anxiety. Because of the direct and intimate sentiments it elicits, this type of trigger is highly potent. From the point their doctors diagnose them, individuals with serious health problems may worry about their condition's progression and how they will cope with the necessary changes that recovery might require. They may also have a hard time accepting their diagnosis. All these worries and fears can induce or worsen anxiety in individuals.

Conflict

Misunderstandings are another trigger for anxiety. A disagreement with a coworker, parent, spouse, child, or even a random individual in a clothing store, can send one spiraling down the road to anxiety.

People who have been bullied at school or work may find it challenging to spend time there because they would be trying their best to avoid conflict and protect themselves. The fear of being bullied can cause some individuals to lose focus on their schoolwork or workload. In learning environments, the victims or those susceptible to being bullied may avoid the place entirely, hindering their learning process.

While it's common to experience work-related stress and anxiety occasionally, it's unusual to remain a daily aspect of the job for months or years. A hostile job or work environment can also trigger anxiety in working-class individuals. From stormy workplace relationships to unfavorable working conditions, one may find themself anxious about change.

Lifestyle Habits

In many cases, it is highly probable that when one is constantly worried about every this and that crossing their mind, they may be doing it to themself. Yes, that's right.

Several people rely on their morning cup of coffee to get through busy days, which may cause or exacerbate anxiety. Recent findings agree that people with panic disorder and social anxiety disorder are susceptible to the anxiety-inducing effects of caffeine (Klevebrant & Frick, 2022). In reasonable doses, coffee is beneficial, albeit tolerance levels vary depending on the metabolic system of each individual. Caffeine overdose can negatively affect certain people, worsening their anxiety symptoms.

How does that even work? Caffeine increases the plasma concentration of *epinephrine*, one of the hormones that facilitate the fight-or-flight response. Now, think about it: Every *typical* morning as you leave for work after that morning coffee, you have your senses on high alert, and your mind is ready to fly you away if there's any danger, but are there any signs of impending danger? Unless you work in a high-risk industry, remember it's a typical day, meaning you should arrive at your workplace in one piece. Suppose you are drinking several cups of coffee a day. In that case, however, your mind will constantly be worrying about possible accidents, how to respond if you get fired, what to do if you lose an important contract, and many other thoughts of adverse events that don't happen on one-coffee days.

Irregular eating habits are another lifestyle flaw that can trigger anxiety in some people. Your blood sugar may drop if you don't eat enough food to support the various processes necessary for healthy living. Eating well-balanced meals is essential for a variety of reasons. It gives you energy as well as essential nutrients. When you skip meals, your blood sugar levels drop, opening doors to many unfavorable symptoms such as trembling hands, pounding heartbeat, dizziness, and many others. Healthy snacks are an excellent method to prevent low blood sugar, agitation, or anxiousness if your circumstances do not favor three meals a day.

Personal Triggers

These triggers are prevalent in individuals with *post-traumatic stress disorder*, a mental health problem in people with past traumatic experiences. Although they can be difficult for others to spot, personal anxiety triggers remind you of a painful memory or traumatic experience in your life, consciously or unintentionally. It could start with a smell, a location, or even a familiar sound that doesn't sit well with you. If you have personal anxiety triggers, you may find that some places, such as hospitals, libraries, or even particular areas such as your backyard, make you uncomfortable and may trigger unwelcome emotions from the past.

Self-Neglect

As much as we may want to avoid talking about poor self-care as if it doesn't exist, it is yet another surprising anxiety trigger. Neglecting and failing to meet your personal needs might cause you to worry. It's vital to review your self-care behaviors and attempt to do better by yourself—the small things such as grooming regularly, eating balanced meals, and getting enough sleep matter. Constant trouble doing these chores could signal something more concerning, such as depression, which tends to coexist with anxiety.

A cluttered home environment can also have a significant impact on the life of someone who suffers from anxiety. Shocking, right? Several people gape at the idea that disorderly living spaces can trigger anxiety. When your home is untidy, thoughts that you should clean and organize things in and around the house can linger in your mind, leading to symptoms such as decreased concentration, increased tension, and other unhealthy symptoms for someone with anxiety problems.

Life itself is another uncertain phenomenon, and uncertainty triggers anxiety. Becoming a parent, for example, is a life-changing experience with countless thrilling possibilities. However, parenting can be difficult and overly draining, which often causes a great deal of tension and anxiety. Parents-to-be might be worried about how they'll adjust to their new role. They might be concerned about the birth itself, the baby's health afterward, and their responsibilities as new parents.

Grief is another life change that contributes to mental unwellness in many people. It is often associated with profound feelings of grief and melancholy. In many circumstances, the loss comes with severe anxiety. People may experience increased pressure following the death of someone they were close to. A suffering individual may be concerned about how they will move forward without their loved one. Several people also worry about coping with their loss and may have challenges feeling normal again. Some worry about their work, studies, or business due to losing concentration while dealing with grief.

You and Anxiety

Besides the trembling and dizziness that anxiety can cause in individuals; it also can interrupt bodily systems, disturbing natural processes, especially those that have to do with mental health. In this section, we will discuss the effects of anxiety on human well-being.

Mental Health

Anxiety and panic attacks that last for a long time can lead your brain to release stress chemicals regularly, making symptoms such as headaches and dizziness occur very frequently.

When you're anxious or agitated, your brain sends hormones and other chemicals to your neurological system to trigger a response to possible threats. Examples of stress hormones include cortisol and adrenaline. While the hormones can be beneficial for high-stress occurrences that happen occasionally, long-term exposure to them can be detrimental to your physical health.

Memory Loss

Chronic anxiety can compromise your memory, leading to problems such as failing to keep up with daily schedules, forgetting necessary appointments, and making many mistakes. When this occurs regularly, you may find it difficult to make critical decisions at work or home, and performance at school or work may also be compromised.

Weight Gain

When you become nervous, your brain releases adrenaline and cortisol hormones into your body. Repeated exposure to the hormones is likely to make you crave sweet comfort foods such as creamy pastries, chocolates, or cakes, all of which are unhealthy in large quantities. Most of these foods contain simple sugars, a quality that makes them very easy for the body to digest and use, leaving you hungry shortly after. On the other hand, this surge and subsequent decline in blood sugar levels results in stubborn cravings for salty and sweet meals. Continuous, uncontrolled eating can lead to weight gain and, eventually, obesity, among other serious health complications.

Alcohol and Drug Abuse

If you ask someone how they deal with difficult emotions, you will find quite a few who resort to alcohol and mood-altering substances. Why is that so?

Some substances have short-term anxiety-relieving properties, and some people who have trouble controlling their fears find consolation in the substance. Some are taken with food or drinks, others smoked, and others simply require that the user gets a whiff and sit back as all their worries disappear. Although it is true such substances exist, they do not exactly toss your worries off the planet.

At least not forever. The dangers of substance abuse outweigh any temporary relief of thoughts.

Another problem with alcohol and drugs as a way to escape anxiety is addiction. Alcohol and drugs can easily make it a habit to rely on them to avoid dealing with fears face-to-face. Uncontrolled, constant exposure to drugs and alcohol can lead to a degree of dependency that leaves the individual unable to cope on their own.

Chapter 2:

The Damage Done

Have you suffered anxiety due to the COVID-19 pandemic? Many people lost their friends and families, others lost businesses and some lost their jobs. Can you relate? Most people can. It is easy to relate because the impact of the pandemic is widespread, with no regard for race, level of education, or social status. The COVID-19 pandemic remains a worldwide health concern, stirring a range of emotions, from grief to despair. The sudden changes and uncertainties that come with such a widespread health challenge are disturbing and have a significant impact on mental health. In this chapter, we will discuss some of the negative ways in which the pandemic has interfered with the familiar normal, causing a major disruption that has triggered pandemic anxiety in several individuals.

COVID-19 and Employment

One day you have a well-paying job to maintain your needs as well as support those in your life, the next your job is no longer secure, and after that, it is gone. The loss of employment as a result of companies and factories closing down temporarily or permanently caused countless job shortages throughout the world. This crisis poses a great danger of food shortages, increasing poverty as well as a decrease in the provision of several important resources. The damage is so significant that individuals may continue to suffer from the impact for years to come.

The COVID-19 pandemic has affected different groups of workers to varying extents. While certain policies adopted by governments in different countries have helped cushion the impact, the crisis has nevertheless exacerbated some existing inequalities in the labor market, disproportionately affecting already-disadvantaged groups such as the poorly educated, young people, and some ethnic groups. There are countless groups of people whose finances were already shaky before the pandemic, and now they don't stand a chance to balance their financial affairs.

State-imposed lockdowns and closures of firms have left millions of people unsure of what the future holds for them. As the pandemic was spreading around the world, many workplaces closed down. Millions of workers lost all of their income and others had to accept shorter hours and settle for wage cuts in different industries. In some instances, employers negotiated wage cuts in collective agreements with their workers, leaving little to no room for fancy choices because many other individuals would have eyes on the same job.

Amidst the pandemic, most companies resorted to having their employers work from home. This means that people who were already vulnerable, for instance, those with poor knowledge of technological systems, new entrants, or individuals in remote areas were at risk of being laid off. From a business standpoint, it's understandable because retraining and upskilling these vulnerable workers would take time and a lot of money, but what about them? What about their families?

If you or someone close to you recently lost a formal job or had to close down a business that was once productive, how did you deal with the negative emotions that followed? What about the fear of moving forward without a reliable source of income?

COVID-19 and Education

The unprecedented public health crisis that resulted from the coronavirus pandemic also led to the emergency closure of educational institutions. Many of us thought it was only going to last a few weeks, but as those weeks became months, rapid transitions from traditional learning methods to digital solutions also became necessary for some progress in education sectors throughout the world.

Despite efforts to mitigate the impact of COVID-19 on education, numerous exam candidates suffered delays and disorganization in various learning institutions. Their examinations had to be postponed, again, and again. Students from less privileged backgrounds also experienced major setbacks due to the outbreak. Reduction in family income, limited access to digital resources, and the high cost of internet connectivity disrupted their academic lives, depriving them of basic education. Although we are in the 21st century, there are still many people from various parts of the world, who lack basic knowledge in technological operations, and others who have it can't even afford access. How do students from such backgrounds cope?

The pandemic has also affected public spending on education as funds were diverted into the health and economic sectors. The slowdown of economic growth associated with the spread of the virus impacted the availability of public funding for education. There were interruptions in higher education as universities closed their premises and countries shut their borders in response to lockdown measures for public health. This crisis affected the progression of learning and the delivery of course material, as well as the safety and legal status of international students in their host countries.

The negative effect of the coronavirus outbreak also impacted students' perception of the value of their academic achievements. Several students became hopeless with time, while others had to quit because of desperation. There are instances of students dropping out of tertiary education programs in search of more promising ventures or just anything that can bring tangible benefits. Imagine having spent years studying to build your career, then the pandemic closes in just as you are about to finish, disturbing your schedule and finances, and even threatening your safety. How would you carry on? If you can relate, regardless of your reason for giving up on your academic plans, the fact remains that the coronavirus outbreak had a widespread effect on the education system, and the uncertainty remains a cause for concern. Surely you can feel anxious when you don't know if and how you will resume your studies. It is unsettling to realize just how much we do not have control over what we once thought we did. So how do we proceed?

COVID-19 and Healthcare

The coronavirus pandemic caused a change in the priorities of medical and surgical procedures. Various individuals who wanted some healthcare services could not get it as quickly as they anticipated due to postponement, and sometimes even cancellation of elective surgeries and non-urgent medical care. The outbreak also caused many healthcare systems to skip their routine tests in an effort to cope with health service demand. Several individuals had difficulties accessing hospitals and those with chronic diseases had to postpone their follow-ups as hospital access was mostly limited to urgent cases. As if postponement wasn't bad enough, some of the patients didn't even show up after the given time elapsed. In some individuals, this led to further medical complications as a result of unaddressed health concerns. Other people unnecessarily suffered pain to such an extent that they lost all the hope they had and bombarded themselves with questions like, "What's the point?"

Because the effect of the outbreak was widespread, developing countries had limited access to treatment from other countries. The decrease in the provision of medical supplies worsened the burden on the health care systems in such countries. Although the idea behind lockdowns and other measures was to fight the outbreak, this resulted in the system neglecting the fight against other diseases such as tuberculosis and HIV.

The high number of critically ill, admitted patients, against a few healthcare providers led to exhaustion and burnout that resultantly caused inefficient service delivery. Several health workers got infected with the virus and some lost their lives, further reducing the available manpower and compromising the efficiency of the healthcare system.

If you have had someone close to you suffer from any of these healthcare challenges, you could find yourself worried about their safety and yours. People often wonder, "What if it only gets worse?"

COVID-19 and Social Interactions

Some of the elements stemming from the outbreak cause increased depression levels in individuals and challenges such as anxiety are certain to occur frequently. These problems include, but are not limited to, separation from loved ones and loss of freedom. In efforts to reduce and prevent further damage, we had to observe quarantine, social distancing, and other safety measures that interfered with social interactions. The level of uncertainty about the advancement of the coronavirus disease causes a significant degree of helplessness and an insurmountable fear regarding what's to come.

Despite social networking being an effective way to cope with difficult times, authorities had to limit physical interactions to minimize the chances of the disease spreading, which left most people without outlets for their emotions.

COVID-19 and Stigmatization

Social stigma in the context of health is the negative association toward people who share certain characteristics or a specific disease. Stigmatization hurts those with the disease, as well as their caregivers, family, friends, and communities. During this coronavirus outbreak, various people were labeled, stereotyped, and discriminated against. Some people were treated separately, and others lost their social status because of a perceived link with the disease. Various individuals from different parts of the world were unfairly subjected to verbal and in some cases, even physical abuse due to misplaced beliefs that their ethnicity was associated with the virus. These challenges caused people to avoid being tested or taking necessary protection measures. Deeper than that, stigmatization during the coronavirus outbreak also contributed to social isolation as the labeled individuals had to distance themselves from others to avoid judgment and conflict. Among the negative impacts of that lack of social interaction lurks pandemic anxiety.

The stigma associated with COVID-19 is mainly due to the disease being new and the plethora of unknowns that surround the subject. To help address the stigma, it is important to show empathy toward those affected. You can also learn and understand more about the disease itself to avoid wrongfully making others feel uncomfortable.

The Impact of COVID-19 on Anxiety

The pandemic has had a significant impact on mental well-being. Many people with anxiety have had to deal with worsened symptoms and some who didn't have anxiety issues before the outbreak had to learn and adjust to the scary times in which we are living. From news headlines, and buzzing rumors in packed neighborhoods, to isolated living conditions, it is easy to get lost in thoughts, wondering about many questions to which no one has answers as of yet. In this section, we will take a closer look at how the coronavirus pandemic impacted anxiety both in people who already had mental difficulties and in those who did not.

Grief

> *Grief is like the ocean; it comes on waves ebbing and flowing. Sometimes the water is calm, and sometimes it is overwhelming. All we can do is learn to swim.* –Vicki Harrison

When we lose something or someone dear to us, it is normal to experience a time of deep sorrow in response to the loss. This kind of loss is different from losing car keys or forgetting where you put your bank cards. Grief is deeper. It is intense. People often grieve following serious life events that leave them emotionally distressed, such as divorce, a sudden dismissal from work, the death of a loved one, and many other painful events.

In relation to the coronavirus disease outbreak, the most common trigger for grief is the death of a friend or family member. If you have lost someone close to you during this difficult time, you may have gone through a period of emotional suffering as you tried to cope with the loss. Different individuals grieve in different ways. While others may isolate themselves and avoid external interaction, others dive into social interaction to try and forget their sorrow. In the same way, different people have different ways of dealing with emotional hardships, and the time it takes to grieve also varies from person to person. Some individuals need to take time to even realize their loss and understand what it means, others stay in denial, hoping to wake up the next day and find their loved one in good health. A few other people quickly understand that the loss is beyond their control and they quickly move on. If you have or are experiencing grief after losing a friend or family member, it is important to remember that grieving doesn't mean you are emotionally weak, but it is a normal part of life.

The coronavirus disease outbreak's impact on anxiety through grief is mainly about people losing their loved ones to respiratory difficulties or other causes of death that are directly linked to the pandemic. Even if one hasn't lost someone close to them, just seeing others in pain after the death of their loved ones can trigger fear, worry, and some degree of mental discomfort. People may worry about the safety of their friends, families, and others who are close to them. Worried individuals may live in fear of the day the outbreak causes them that much pain as well. In these kinds of instances, worried individuals may say things such as:

- That could have been anyone.

- That could have been us.

- We are not safe here

- Nothing is guaranteed.

- Will this ever end?

- When will this end?

Denial

Denial is like a cloud that obscures the sky. It blocks the truth. It reduces clarity. –Gloria Excelsior

Another way by which the coronavirus pandemic impacts anxiety in individuals after they lose their loved ones is through denial. Loss is a painful ordeal and it's not always the case that people accept it as it is and move on thereafter. While some individuals do take time to heal by grieving, others do not even take the first step toward healing. If one does not understand or chooses to ignore their loss as if everything is as it should be, they take a long time to heal and will most certainly need immense help throughout the process. In these kinds of situations, the individuals at loss refuse to believe that their loved one is gone, or that their friend or family member is unwell, with low chances of recovery. They tend to convince themselves that they will just wake up someday and everything will be normal again.

This false reality that they create for themselves hinders them from working on the real challenges toward their healing journey. When reality finally sinks in, the truth can be so overwhelming that they get anxious and start battling other mental health challenges such as mood fluctuations and uncharacteristic behaviors.

Despair

The formula for despair comes from when we suffer, and choose not to see the meaning in the suffering. Therefore despair equals suffering with the absence of meaning. —Viktor Frankl

When confronted by something as serious, yet unfamiliar as the coronavirus outbreak, it is understandable that several people may feel out of control. In this difficult time, however, there comes a point at which the realization of having little to no say in an individual's health issues or the lives of their loved ones becomes excessively overwhelming. Some individuals worry when they realize that they can't do much for their loved ones. This realization isn't only heartbreaking, but it can also cause people to feel anxious during difficult times.

Another problem that affects anxiety as a result of the coronavirus outbreak is an increase in the cost of medication. In some areas, the concern isn't even money, but a widespread shortage of treatments. When friends, caregivers, and family members toil in search of medication but to no avail, they may run out of hope at some point.

When people realize that they can't do much to help their friend or family member, some decide to stay positive and hope for better, but others sulk in despair. The individuals who despair when faced with hard times usually feel as though they don't need to hold on because in their mind, what they do can't change a thing. When one loses hope, they may ask themselves questions such as:

- "Why does it even matter?"
- "Why bother?"

Continuously pondering over such matters can cause mental unrest and worsen symptoms of anxiety.

Relationship Tension

The unpredictable nature of the coronavirus outbreak causes tension in some relationships. Due to loss of employment, some family ties become fragile as family members worry about income. If a family had one breadwinner and that person loses their job, others would have to step up to support the family, or they can decide to live on emergency savings while they figure out what to do next. With the coronavirus outbreak, however, having someone else step up is easier said than done because the impact of the pandemic on the economy requires most people to adopt new ways of making money. For people who only understand the traditional workplace environment, immediate adaptation is almost impossible so the whole family ends up stuck at home, with no source of income. Financial hurdles bring misunderstandings that are strong enough to tear families apart, and that can worsen feelings of anxiety during the pandemic.

Another way in which the outbreak impacts anxiety in relationships is by forcing people to be together even when they would rather spend some time apart to think and sort out their issues. Different people have different personalities. Some people naturally love spending time with their families and friends, others prefer to spend most of their time alone, and some would rather stay at their workplace even on weekends and holidays! Although each group has reasons to justify their preferences, adjusting to staying at home daily can prove challenging for most people who enjoy being outdoors. Because the effects of the pandemic can force people out of their jobs and send them home, some people have had to keep up with family affairs regardless of whether or not they like it. While that can be a good thing when looking at it with the idea that it gives people time to bond and a chance to resolve differences, that isn't always the case. Sometimes people have to wait misunderstandings out until they gather the energy to discuss and solve their problems. Talking about such issues before they are ready, but only because they happen to be at the same place, with little to do or talk about may only increase tension between individuals. In these settings, one may become anxious about the probability of more complex problems such as divorce.

Life Hardships

There are times when problems seem to communicate, signaling each other to pour in at once or in tandem. In such instances, one requires resilience to not give up and just let things just become whichever way they turn out. The situation needs someone who will stand and fight, but even the strong run out of strength sometimes. The coronavirus pandemic doesn't make such situations any easier. Although this depends on one's attitude, in many people's eyes, the outbreak opens doors for more problems. When difficulties come flying before one's face, the individual can become anxious about whether they will ever find peace.

Chapter 3:

Ways to Cope

Fighting anxiety starts with you, it starts from within. You can try pain medications and sedatives, but none of that will help if you do not look after yourself. The various strategies for easing anxiety will only suffice if you are determined to go the extra mile and take charge of your health. Ways of fighting anxiety during the pandemic slightly differ from before, when we could go shopping to clear our minds. That is why the following chapters will guide you through every step of the way. In this chapter, we will focus on the basics of self-care, ways to practice it, as well as steps to create your personalized self-care strategy.

Self-Care

When you take purposeful action to improve your emotional, mental, and physical well-being and ensure a healthy lifestyle, what you are practicing is called self-care, an important technique for enhancing mental health. Contrary to common perception, self-care is not a luxury; it's a necessity!

You can practice self-care in a variety of ways, such as getting adequate sleep, engaging in physical activities, and giving yourself a break. Self-care is essential for developing resilience to some hardships of life that are beyond your control, such as the coronavirus outbreak. Once you take genuine efforts to care for your body and mind, you will be more at peace with yourself and experience better mental clarity.

People who neglect their well-being become overwhelmed and exhausted. They are also unequipped to deal with life's inevitable obstacles. Unwinding isn't the only aspect of self-care. Reviewing your self-care practices in various areas of life is critical to ensure that you care for your soul, body, and mind. You must also strike a balance to address each of these areas as you improve your health and well-being. Restore balance or find respite from a stressor in your life, you may require more self-care in one area than the other, but that should be easier to implement once you understand the essence of self-care.

Physical Self-Care

Your body and mind have an inextricable link, which means taking care of your mind requires you to take care of your body. Physical self-care is about how much sleep you get, how you fuel your body, how physically active you are, and how well you look after your physical requirements. It includes things such as attending your hospital appointments as scheduled, taking medication as prescribed, and keeping track of your health.

Balance Your Diet

The food choices you make either promote your health or compromise it. Bad food choices can make you more receptive to mental health challenges such as stress and anxiety. Although resorting to comfort foods that are rich in fat and sugar may offer you a distraction and short-term relief from anxiety, they will only add to your mental and physical health problems in the long run. Sweets and cookies, for example, trigger a blood sugar increase almost immediately after you swallow them down. Your body then uses the energy just as quickly, then your blood glucose levels drop. The resultant decrease in blood sugar levels then causes you to feel stressed and anxious.

Ensuring that you eat a balanced diet improves mental clarity and helps keep you healthy. Nutritious foods such as vegetables, fruits, and nuts help manage mood fluctuations. Healthy food does not mean expensive food, so even with the coronavirus pandemic still at large, you can eat healthily. Vegetables such as carrots, lettuce, and cucumbers are easy to grow in your backyard or home garden. Although you may have to buy some of your grains and proteins, once you plan out your diet, you can adjust for simplicity and affordability.

Exercise

Physical activity is essential for mental health improvement and management. The best part is that there are a variety of activities to help you relax. Workouts are excellent for alleviating anxiety symptoms and they can be as flexible as you like. Exercise ranges from simple activities such as walks to heavy workouts that require more energy. Your choice of exercise depends on factors such as flexibility, your desired outcome, the amount of time you have, your mood at that given moment, and various other factors.

Walks allow you to experience a change of environment, which helps you relax and get into a better frame of mind while giving you the benefits of exercise at the same time. You can take a short walk around your house, job, school or just in your neighborhood. It doesn't have to be exhausting or in crowded places, you just want something peaceful and relaxing.

Yoga incorporates physical movement and meditation. It also helps control your breathing, even when you have problems focusing or calming down. All of these benefits have a positive impact on your mental and general well-being. You do not have to leave your home to practice yoga, you can have sessions at home, and even better, with your family members. If you have never tried yoga before, you could start by looking up some free classes on the internet. If you already have some experience but just need more guidance or encouragement, you can make use of some applications that will take you through a session with calm music to help you relax.

Regulate Your Sleep Patterns

Another important practice for mental well-being is exercising good sleep hygiene. Sleep too is a necessity, not a luxury. Despite its many benefits, getting proper sleep can be problematic for several individuals. While both too much and too little sleep have negative impacts on your anxiety and overall well-being, sleep deprivation is a major concern during hard times.

Several people who experience sleep deprivation either fail to fall sleep, sleep restfully or they have trouble staying asleep. The factors that affect sleep quality range from trivial changes such as your sleep attire to grave concerns such as depression, anxiety, and other health conditions. In this section, we will take a look into some of these factors to help you determine areas of your lifestyle that need improvement.

Anxiety

The relationship between sleep and anxiety is rather fascinating. Anxiety can lead to sleep deprivation, and sleep deprivation can exacerbate anxiety. As if that's not enough, some of the medications for fighting anxiety and other mental health issues can interfere with your sleep patterns and increase your anxiety.

Sharing The Bed

Sometimes individuals share their beds with babies or pets, but this habit can compromise sleep quality. Sharing a bed with a partner who snores or makes uncomfortable movements can also disturb your sleep. Another problem with sharing the bed with an adult partner is that they may have different preferences for their sleep environment. This includes lighting, temperature, and other such factors.

Drinking Alcohol

Consumption of alcohol in large amounts before your bedtime can disturb your sleep cycle. Drinking too much alcohol before bed interferes with your sleep, causing challenges in falling asleep or staying asleep. Consuming too much alcohol before bed can also cause you to oversleep and it will likely be unrestful.

Irregular Sleep Patterns

Sometimes poor sleep habits such as sleeping too early and staying up too late contribute to poor sleep quality. Going to sleep earlier than you normally would disturbs your usual sleep schedule. If you normally sleep for seven hours, for instance, sleeping two hours earlier might not add up to nine hours, but you may wake up two hours earlier than usual. An important question is—then what? Chances are you may try to sleep another two hours, which is possible, just expensive if you want to improve the quality of your sleep. Your body and mind will remember that you slept two hours early, and in the future, they may entice you to bed two hours early, or you may find yourself awake before it is time. The same concept applies to staying up or going to bed too late.

Screen Time

Exposure to light at bedtime interferes with your quality of sleep. The light could be from your lamp, smartphone, television, or other devices and light sources. Spending time on your smartphone or gaming computer during or just before bedtime can make you sleepless, or cause interruptions after you fall asleep.

Regardless of what impairs your sleep, we can take various practical steps to improve sleep hygiene by developing and sticking to proper sleep regimens. One of the most important steps toward regulating sleep is developing consistency. Try incorporating the following strategies to improve the quality of your sleep.

- Avoid eating and drinking two to three hours before bed.

- Maintain the same sleep routine every day, making sure you get enough sleep each night.

- Invest in comfortable bedding because a poorly built mattress or old pillow can interrupt your sleep as well as cause other physical health problems such as neck and back pain.

- Avoid hot room temperatures as too much heat can interrupt your sleep cycle or cause you to oversleep.

- Use heavy drapes or shades to block off light, and earplugs to drown out disturbing sounds.

- Try keeping your bedroom tidy and clutter-free.

- Abstain from using your bedroom for watching TV, eating, reading, studying, gaming, internet browsing, or any other activities that are not sleep-related.

- You can also use calming candles or scents such as lavender or chamomile to help you relax before bed.

Emotional Self-Care

The ability to control your emotions and how you handle different life experiences is called emotional wellness. This awareness plays a significant role in regulating your mental well-being.

Relationships

Social interactions require us to define and understand our motives and perspectives regarding various issues. How one deals with disagreements determines whether or not one can maintain positive relationships that last. If you have trouble controlling your emotions and calmly resolving conflicts, you may encounter difficulties dealing with other people. It wouldn't be a problem if we didn't need other people for our sanity. Still, we need a few friends to rely on to maintain our well-being while fighting anxiety, especially during this challenging time of the Covid-19 pandemic.

Before one invests much in building friendships or other kinds of relationships, they must reach within themself to determine how they feel and what they expect in the relationship, as well as consider how the relationship benefits both parties involved. Knowing what to expect in any kind of relationship helps minimize unprogressive arguments, risks of being disappointed, and any other unfavorable situations that may arise during your connection. Many people who do not give their relationships enough thought in the beginning end up sad, stressed, or alone. You do not want to lose a friend during this time of hardship.

Mental Health

When going through difficult situations such as the aftermath of the coronavirus outbreak, mental wellness is more important than ever. The relationship between mental and emotional wellness is strong and if you neglect it, you may grow weary and anxious. Because the pandemic may trigger various conflicting emotions in you, it is important that you learn and work on how to face these issues.

Emotional self-care involves taking part in activities that encourage you to appreciate and express how you feel about different situations positively and safely. Different individuals have different self-care practices depending on various factors such as affordability and accessibility. Given the current situation worldwide, accessibility is of great importance when picking out activities for self-care because if you pick an option that requires you to mingle in crowded places, not only do you expose yourself to biased updates that can trigger your anxiety, but you also risk contracting the virus.

Below are some useful strategies you can use to regulate your emotions and stay out of several situations that are otherwise emotionally draining.

Label the Feeling

We often avoid feeling what we are feeling, but identifying our emotions at any stressful moment is the first step toward dealing with the feelings in question. Putting a name to the emotions disturbing you gives you clarity and direction. You cannot work toward feeling better if you do not know how bad you feel in the first place. Once you pinpoint what you feel, you can trace it back to recent or easy events that could have caused you to feel that way. You can journal what you feel to create a pattern that you can refer back to. You can also talk to a friend or someone trustworthy about what you feel. They can help you sort through your emotions, giving you a better chance to work them out and feel better.

Determine if Your Feelings Are Productive or Unproductive

Although emotions are not always black or white, they either help you progress, or not. Anxiety is an excellent example of how the same emotions can have different impacts in different situations. When anxiety helps you realize you are not ready for your exam and forces you out of bed to study, it is productive and helpful. If you miss your exam because you are too scared of failing it, that becomes a weak emotion.

This applies to several kinds of emotions, if not all, so we would be wrong to assume that feelings are either bad or good. However, we can describe the impact of particular emotions as either positive or negative. You can determine strategies to manage emotions that have a negative effect while maintaining those with a positive impact.

Embrace The Feeling

Some emotions are not worth sulking over, sometimes you just have to acknowledge what you are going through and get over it. Minor disturbances in mood usually subside on their own. If, for example, someone bumped into you and spilled water on your shoe, you can get a little upset about having to wipe the shoes, but this is not something you should hold on to for the rest of the week.

To effectively determine emotions that usually go away on their own, calculate how the emotions are affecting your well-being and if they are interfering with your thoughts. If not, they are probably usual day-to-day inconveniences that come and go.

Practice Healthy Coping Strategies

Although some people numb, ignore or suppress their emotions, one needs to experiment with coping strategies until they find what works best for them. Suppressing your emotions doesn't help your self-care practices, and it doesn't help with your anxiety or other mental health challenges either. Denying how you are feeling can help calm you down or brighten your mood for a short time, but that is all it does. You will still have the same challenges when you get up the next day or when you recollect yourself enough to go to bed where no one is watching you.

Some people take on strategies such as cooking, talking, writing, or even taking a warm bath, others just relax and play music. As long as you know that what works for your friend might not work for you, you have a high chance of getting your emotional self-care practices back on track!

Stay alert to avoid unhealthy coping practices that may cause new challenges in your life, or worsen your symptoms over time. Overeating can lead to more problems such as obesity or high blood pressure. Depending on drug use for comfort can lead to addiction and other mental health issues.

Social Self-Care

Sometimes it is difficult to make time for friends, and given the current situation, overlooking your relationships can be tempting. Socialization, however, is an integral part of self-care, and if you are determined to fight anxiety through better self-care practices, you will need to clean off some rust and keep all your social ties intact. Although the coronavirus outbreak makes it quite risky to meet up with your friends now and then, you can still stay in touch through digital solutions such as video calls.

Your ability to maintain close relationships determines the quality of your mental health. Investing time and energy into developing and maintaining close ties with those around you is the best strategy to nurture and sustain your relationships. You should spend no set amount of time with your friends or family. If you want to repair old ties, you may have to spend a little more time and effort to rekindle dying flames. If you want to maintain relationships that are already stable, all you have to do is keep the wheel wheeling.

Whether it is a relationship between you and your child, parent, friend, or spouse, the following features of healthy relationships hold true and the provided strategies will help improve the life expectancy of your relationship.

Qualities of Positive Relationships

Perfect relationships are a myth, they do not exist outside fantasy movies and novels. Every relationship has its share of flaws, but what makes it worth holding on to is that each individual recognizes the work that their relationship requires to survive, and is ready to fight through the stormy days and nights.

Everyone's social needs are different, but the idea is to figure out yours and those of your loved ones, then you make it work. Some of the following values constitute a positive relationship, one that is worth rebuilding or maintaining:

- respect
- discussing dreams and fears
- support
- honesty
- fairness
- maintaining individual identity
- trust
- affection

For various reasons specific to the individual in question, your child, friend, family, or spouse may need more of one or two of these qualities than the rest. If one has trouble trusting people, they may require you to constantly show them they can rely on you. If you are constantly worried about your relationship or other matters, you may need more time to discuss your fears with them.

Trust

One seed that fuels every positive relationship is trust. Every healthy relationship requires you to have faith in the other individual and vice versa. Although previous relationships shape your expectations for current and future relationships, if your current relationship is healthy, you can work to put adverse effects from previous relationships behind you. You are more likely to trust your partner if you perceive that they treat you well, are reliable, and will be there for you when you need them.

You are more inclined to trust prospective partners if your previous relationships were secure, stable, and trusting. If, on the other hand, your previous relationships were unstable and unreliable, you may have to work through trust issues in the future. This usually applies to relationships with family, spouses, and friends, not necessarily parent-child relationships.

Establishing trust in a relationship necessitates mutual self-disclosure through exchanging personal information. With the progression of time, more opportunities to put that trust to the test and evaluate it arise. If you succeed, your relationship becomes a huge source of security and comfort. However, if you feel compelled to keep secrets in your relationship, you may lack this crucial quality.

Honesty

Although every relationship's level of openness differs, you should never feel obligated to hide elements of yourself. If your relationship is healthy, you should feel free to be authentic. Honesty strengthens your bonds in a relationship and nurtures and improves trust. Holding back and exercising more caution about sharing information in the early stages of your relationship is common. Still, as it grows, you loosen up and share more of your beliefs, thoughts, opinions, memories, and hobbies.

The need for openness in relationships does not imply that you must disclose everything to your partner. Each person requires personal space and solitude. The important thing that counts most is whether you are at ease communicating your fears, emotions, and hopes with your partner.

While your friend's or partner's needs may differ from yours, working on ways to compromise for them while maintaining your personal limits is critical. Do not manipulate boundaries in favor of secrecy, but use them to ensure you both have your freedom. When implemented the right way and used as intended, personal edges reduce the chances of one partner suffocating in the relationship. This buffer is especially important given that some people now have to spend more time with each other than they did before the pandemic.

Mutual Respect

Individuals who are in close, healthy relationships appreciate one another. They provide support and assurance for each other without mocking or discouraging one another.

People in positive relationships can practice respect for one another in various ways, such as:

- listening to each other
- showing empathy
- forgiving each other
- accommodating each other's needs and dreams
- sharing constructive ideas while supporting each other's individuality

Proper Communication

Communication skills are necessary for all types of relationships, including romantic, familial, and friendly ones. Although it may seem that the finest relationships are ones that are free of conflict, knowing how to settle disagreements is more vital than just avoiding conflicts to keep the peace. When friends or family members bottle up emotions to keep the peace, they are likely to explode, suffocate, or drown. Whichever happens will negatively impact the relationship, and depending on how the involved individuals resolve the situation, the relationship can crumble and die.

If you can handle it well, conflict is sometimes a chance to improve your relationship with your partner. It allows you to make necessary adjustments for the progression of your relationship. You learn to talk about your feelings and ideas and try to devise a compromise while maintaining respect and compassion.

Genuine Affection

Fondness and affection constitute positive relationships. The individuals involved must maintain compassion, tenderness, and comfort, even as their relationship ages. Again, there is no right amount of affection because every individual has varied physical requirements. As long as the parties involved are happy with the amount of affection they share with their friends, spouses, or families, their relationship can prove to be healthy.

How to Build Healthy Relationships

Toxic habits usually indicate that a toxic relationship is in its staggering stages. When your relationship struggles with balance, you can take some steps to restore and maintain stability. Numerous approaches exist to strengthen relationships and address other social issues that may arise.

Show Appreciation

Families or friends who express gratitude toward each other feel well-connected and are happy in their relationships. Even parent-child relationships require you to show appreciation when it is due. That way, the person you are grateful to realize their worth and feels encouraged to do more.

Keep the Relationship Worth Maintaining

Even with the pandemic affecting relations, life has to go on. Living close to your friends or families may eventually get boring due to repetitive daily activities. Fortunately, it doesn't have to be that way. You can incorporate several interactive activities with your families and friends. You can break out of boring routines and find hobbies that suit you. Give each other space to breathe and find ways to surprise each other—the small things matter. Apart from activities, you can take other practical steps to ensure your loved ones feel how much you value them.

One primary concern involves turning off digital devices to focus on your families or friends. It is easy to get carried away on social media as we seek comfort during this difficult time. Still, if you stop for a minute and think about the person or people sitting right next to you, you may realize you have most of the love you need right there with you, not on some smartphone screen.

Using smartphones and other digital devices becomes necessary when you are away from your loved ones. Considering you still have to make time for them while they do the same, you can schedule calls to spend meaningful time virtually with each other. If it is your child or parent on the other side of the screen, they need to know you still love them, and if they are your friend or spouse, they may need reassurance that you are still as committed to the relationship as before. Remember that no one is immune to anxiety, and it's not enough for your friend or spouse to just know you are alive; they need more.

Dine With Your Loved Ones

Appetite scandals fluctuate during difficult times, but sharing meals with your loved ones can help put you at ease while providing many other beneficial outcomes, such as better eating habits. If you eat with your friends or family, you are less likely to stress eat because you know you have something better to look forward to. They will also appreciate having you at the table because it shows you value their company and appreciate their efforts.

Mental and Spiritual Self-Care

How you think, and the kind of matters you concern yourself with contribute to your psychological and spiritual wellness. Examples of mental self-care include engaging in activities that keep your mind clear and sharp, such as puzzles, learning something new, or reading books you find enjoyable. Spiritual well-being isn't necessarily about prayer and worship. It involves creating or discovering a stronger sense of purpose and nourishing better self-knowledge. Although the choice of spiritual self-care activities varies amongst individuals, observing some spiritual self-care practices is essential. Some people prefer going to a place or worship, others are fine as long as they make time to pray at home, and others would rather spend their self-care time meditating and studying their inner selves. Below are a few examples of what you can do as part of your mental and spiritual self-care routine.

Find Your Interests

Sometimes it can be challenging to identify the things you are enthusiastic about. Not having a clear picture of what you love to do does not mean you don't have interests to explore. Sometimes the things we love doing become part of our lives, and we may not even realize their significance until we look closely or someone points them out. You can also discover your interests by asking for feedback from others, paying attention to compliments, or observing what people think of you. You can scan those observations for patterns and factor out the most recurring activities.

On the other hand, just considering what you enjoy doing will assist you in discovering your passion. Take your hobbies and skills into consideration as you weigh your interests.

Develop Your Skills

Build on your existing skills to improve, and learn new skills to develop. Nurturing your skills helps boost your confidence, allows you to connect with others who are interested in the same activity, and gives you a more pronounced sense of purpose.

You may hesitate or procrastinate your learning project, but hesitation is in human nature, and you have to beat it. If you feel it would be too much, you can start small and improve as you go. You can try household tasks such as cooking or minding a garden. Cooking something new helps you learn about healthy eating habits and develop your own recipes. Tending a garden enables you to discover the different techniques involved and will keep you so busy you won't even have time to worry about the outbreak.

Strengthen Your Relationships

Positive relationships are always crucial. Talking about mental and spiritual well-being gives you a sense of belonging and boosts your self-worth. Good relationships pose an opportunity to share experiences and provide support. When you dedicate time each day to interact with your family, arrange a time to meet up with friends, or visit a loved one who needs support, you give yourself a purpose, and that is important for mental and spiritual development. Be careful, however, not to rely solely on digital solutions for building and maintaining relationships because they can do more damage than good if misused.

Find Your Purpose

The coronavirus outbreak proved to several people that there is more fulfilling to life than careers and money. One needs a purpose, something to believe in, and something to keep one going. We all need something solid to live for, otherwise, all we have will eventually lose meaning. Finding your purpose is a tool for living a healthy, better, and happier life. One of the most practical ways to find meaning in life is giving. This is so because there is always someone in need of help. There is happiness in giving; there is pleasure and satisfaction. Giving is not always about money and material items. The Covid-19 pandemic created shortages in various areas of life. You can spend your free time volunteering in the community, you can make time to teach others a skill you think can be helpful during this period, and you can also volunteer at a care facility. Engaging in such productive activities will build on your sense of purpose and reward you with happiness, knowing you are of service to other people around you.

Practice Mindfulness

When you pay close attention to your feelings, thoughts, and all that surrounds you, you become more aware of yourself and how you relate to your environment. The art of paying attention to what surrounds oneself is called mindfulness. This awareness helps you improve your mental health as well as your spiritual health. You become focused and more concerned about the things that matter in life, giving you an even more defined map of your life. When you have most of your life planned out after accepting things you can't change, your mind will be at peace, and that has a significant positive benefit when fighting anxiety.

Self-Care Plan Strategies

When creating a self-care plan, you will want to customize it to suit your lifestyle and meet your needs. It is essential to learn how to create your self-care strategy because they vary among individuals. One that will work for you has to be designed specifically for you to avoid feeling overwhelmed. You can follow the following steps to develop your customized plan that you can adjust whenever necessary.

- Assess the facets of your life and the main interests you pursue daily. This includes family, relationships, business, or other things. Consider the elements of these areas with which you need the most assistance to improve.

- Figure out how you can deal with the stressors you identified and devise plans to improve in areas of weakness.

- Take baby steps toward your goal. Decide on one easy step you can take forward to take better care of yourself.

Schedule time to concentrate on your self-care needs and prioritize your plans even when it seems impossible to fit anything else in. This is about yourself, after all. You will discover that you can fight most of your anxiety during the pandemic by taking better care of yourself. Another benefit of coming up with a defined plan for taking care of yourself is that you can work more productively and achieve most of your goals once you are at peace with your mental health.

Remember that self-care approaches are specific to every individual and that you must adapt your self-care strategy to fit your requirements and the circumstances in your life at that given time. It is not advisable to postpone working on your problems until you reach your breaking point because it could be too late.

Chapter 4:

Dealing with Anxiety

Fighting anxiety takes work, a lot of it. What makes that statement good news is that fighting anxiety is possible. Everything worth having shouldn't come on a silver plate but should be a result of your hard work and a symbol of your determination. Many people have anxiety and live with it just fine. When you feel like your burden is becoming too heavy, remind yourself that you can get through this. In this chapter, you will discover simple ways to cope with anxiety. Some individuals prefer working on themselves before they can go to their healthcare providers for help. The methods in this chapter are still ideal even if you are taking pharmacological treatment for your anxiety. Find out which methods work best for you in this chapter.

Avoiding Triggers

One of the simplest ways to deal with your anxiety during the COVID-19 pandemic is to avoid situations or activities that trigger you. As previously discussed, these triggers are different for each individual, and so is their impact on one's anxiety. In this chapter, you will learn more about steering clear of activities or situations that may cause or trigger your fears and insecurities.

Frequent COVID-19 Updates

While it is essential always to stay updated, activities such as watching the news or viewing updates about COVID-19 can put you in a flight or fight mode, which can in turn manifest as anxiety. Frequent updates can cause you to panic, and the amount of uncertainty regarding the pandemic will give you a lot to think about, cooking up an intense fear of the unknown. It is essential to control the amount of information you feed or expose yourself to concerning COVID-19. Control and regulate the time you spend watching news updates about COVID-19. If you start feeling heavily disturbed by media reports, you can block out all sorts of updates. If you find it too uncomfortable to stay in your house without knowing what is happening outside, you can set a specific time to watch updates. Remember not to overdo it. This will help calm you and focus your energy on things you can control.

Misinformation

With the rise in usage of the internet, various people spread a lot of conspiracy theories about the coronavirus disease outbreak daily. The problem with that kind of information is that it's not all trustworthy, and most people spreading it cannot verify their sources. This leads to misinformation, which can worsen your anxiety, cause depression, and disturb your sleep patterns, among other symptoms of psychological distress. The conflicts, misunderstandings, and conspiracy theories that people have online can make these symptoms even worse.

The harmful impact of misleading information has been established in several well-publicized situations. For instance, early during the pandemic, several people raised concerns about disinfectant marketing adverts claiming to heal COVID-19 in infected people. What inhumane lies! There are many other lies in circulation even till now, and we wouldn't manage to look into all of them even if we tried. False news can cause doctors to give the wrong doses of medicine, and it can also hurt a person's relationship with their healthcare provider because people can get confused about who to trust. This can lead to a prolonged illness, worsening your anxiety while sowing seeds for depression. To be safe and well-informed, get news updates and reliable information from trusted sources such as the Center for Disease Control (CDC), World Health Organization (WHO), or verified local and international news outlets. Always check your sources if you get information from someplace else.

Official Guidelines

Another trick you can use to control your anxiety during the COVID-19 pandemic is to follow the official guidelines on how we should conduct ourselves and the steps we can take to prevent infection. These are simple activities such as:

- thorough hand washing using soap
- social distancing
- hand sanitization
- abiding by mask recommendations

- avoiding crowded places

While these may seem simple and obvious, the fact that you are doing what you can to help control the spread of the virus will help your mind relax, thereby easing your anxiety. For some people with anxiety disorders and constant worry, if they were to walk out of their home without a face mask, by the time they return thoughts could lead to dread about contracting the illness. Such disturbing thoughts can be mitigated following the recommended guidelines.

Vaccination

You can also avoid triggers by deciding to get the COVID-19 vaccine with your loved ones. Vaccines overall lowers the risk of getting infected by the virus it's intended to prevent. Vaccines can also reduce hospital stays in the unfortunate event that someone gets infected by a virus the vaccine is meant to prevent. It can be very comforting to know that you and your loved ones have some protection from a virus, other than constantly worrying about the probability of getting infected.

Avoiding the Talk

Here is a genius hack to avoid triggering your anxiety during this time of uncertainty without costing you a thing! You don't need to go anywhere or do anything apart from avoiding that biased discussion about the outbreak. If your family and friends keep talking about it, you can openly tell them how you feel and how the topic may trigger your anxiety. You can help make it less awkward by simply bringing up lighter topics.

Refreshing Yourself

Relax your mind and try to stay off your digital gadgets for a while. You can go for a walk and communicate with nature whenever you have the opportunity. A little sunshine, trees, and the peaceful sound of birds singing will soothe your heart and help take your mind off negative ideas.

Addressing Stigmatization

Remember we discussed stigmatization as a result of the coronavirus pandemic? There is more to stigma than spreading discrimination and creating social rifts between people of different statuses. Another form of stigma involves one holding negative beliefs about themself. This is called self-stigmatization. People who have mental illness are more likely to have this problem because they may internalize their disease's widespread stigma. If you have self-stigma, it is essential to face it head-on because it can significantly influence the quality of your life and your mental and physical health. The impact of self-stigma on you depends on how much you judge yourself. It can cause feelings of embarrassment and low self-esteem. It also makes it difficult for you to seek necessary help, making your road to coping with anxiety almost impossible.

Tips to Combat Stigma

Suppose you live in an area where fellow community members are actively encouraging stigma against people with COVID-19. In that case, you could feel less confident if your loved one got infected because that would make you a victim of stigmatization too. Whether you are facing stigmatization from external sources or your mind is cooking it up from within, you are still not entirely doomed. You can take a few simple approaches to help combat stigma and boost your confidence. These tips will guide you toward throwing whatever is fueling feelings of inadequacy out of your life. Remind yourself that you are not alone, whatever you may be going through. It could be anxiety, a recent COVID-19 infection, a misinterpreted link between your ethnicity and the virus, or any other factor. The point is that you are not the first to experience it, and you are not alone.

Gather Information.

Find evidence that invalidates those beliefs if your negativity comes from within you. If, for example, you sometimes think you are unworthy of stability because your anxiety is often overwhelming, you can look closely at the stable relationships you already have in your life and find balance from there.

Pour it Out

Stigmatization often stems from misinformation and misrepresentation of facts. You can encourage those around you to gather more reliable information about the subject that is causing the stigma. Knowing the truth will enable them to actively speak out against stigma. By actively taking part in this, you debunk common misconceptions and misguided beliefs while preparing to cancel out a trigger from the list of situations that make you feel on edge. Suppose someone close to you makes a derogatory remark about someone who suffers from the virus or has roots that originate in places that others have wrongly associated with it. In that case, you should educate them and implement a zero-tolerance policy. This will help even more when you try to teach others outside your circle because change starts with you and those around you.

Share Your Diagnosis

Sometimes people around you may speak ill about your condition not knowing how much it affects you, and they can't know unless you speak up. With mental health problems such as anxiety, however, they may not even know that you have that difficulty. They may eventually find out and make a big deal out of it, so all you have to do is beat them to it! You have nothing to hide, so you can just inform them about your diagnosis. This also allows you to share with them exactly what the diagnosis means for you, and what it could mean for them. That way, they have all the essential facts from the beginning and won't have to spread incorrect rumors. This is only an option to help you cope, but if you are unprepared for the questions that may arise when you tell others about your diagnosis, or what they may do with the information, you can take your time to weigh the idea and only do it when you are ready.

Establish a Support System.

No matter what you do, maintain meaningful connections with others and find ways to gain support. Individuals who suffer from stigmatization still have access to a variety of resources, including educational opportunities and emotional support. The first step you can take toward finding support is connecting with others who are in your situation. People who go through similar ordeals have a way of developing a rapport that could lead to a helpful relationship. They can share different strategies for coping that have worked for them, stories about how they got where they are, and of course, non-judgmental ears to listen to when you face obstacles and can't find your way out.

From peer-to-peer support, you can also seek professional help. Mental health professionals are in the best position to help you chew and digest your emotions regarding stigmatization and anxiety itself. They will also provide you with various proven strategies to overcome your mental health challenges, which brings us to the next section of coping with anxiety.

Professional Help

Anxiety can confine you to a world of irrational fear, devoid of joy, and filled with constant alertness to possible horrors and catastrophes. The effectiveness of your treatment depends on your ability to openly and thoroughly communicate in full honesty with the professional treating you. Despite having gone through years and years of training and holding more years of experience in the field, your treating professional cannot physically get inside your brain to take a history of important bits of information regarding your symptoms, emotions, and lifestyle. They will expect you to disclose this kind of information without any hesitation or fear because, the moment you choose them to help you through your journey, you become a team.

You must invest in finding a reputable professional who knows their way around situations like yours. You can get recommendations from family and friends, fellow individuals who have had or are in similar situations, or you can ask your general practitioner to direct you to someone you can trust. You must have some confidence in the professional working with you because not only will that put you at ease in their presence, but knowing you are in good hands will also lessen your anxiety. You shouldn't feel as though you are suffocating when in the presence of your healthcare provider. While that may sound a little dramatic, it happens very often. Some individuals turn all sweaty when they visit their providers for consultation. Reasons for feeling uncomfortable vary from person to person. Still, if you continue to feel uncomfortable with your provider, how they communicate, or how they work in general, you can consider seeing a different provider.

Note that the problem isn't always on the healthcare provider's part; it could be yours too. If you have similar issues with a different provider the second time, you can consider your own input and thought process. It sometimes happens due to anxiety and some other issues, and the good news is that once you discover that the problem may be on your part, you can take action! Talk to your provider about how you feel or what you observed to start the conversation.

Depending on the severity of your anxiety, you may have to work with several different medical professionals and specialists. If they start you on treatment sooner rather than later, you can also expect to recover soon and have your life back on track. Several resources often advise that people with anxiety seek professional help, but only a few go a step further and explain what that even means. So, who are they?

Primary Care Physician

It's not every time you feel nervous that you have anxiety. Sometimes your fear could be a result of an underlying condition, and other times it isn't even something to worry about. To determine if you have a health problem secretly fueling your symptoms, you will need an examination from your primary care physician. They will rule out other factors that cause anxiety such as hormonal imbalance, certain illnesses, or drug side effects.

If all that is clear, they may diagnose you with an anxiety disorder and suggest that you speak to a mental health expert, such as a therapist, psychologist or a psychiatrist. If you have severe anxiety or if you have another mental health problem such as depression on top of the anxiety, your primary care physician will also point you toward a mental health professional for specialized help. If it turns out you are just nervous about the weather and will be fine the next day, your doctor will clear you to go back home and bake cookies.

Psychologist

When you visit a psychologist, you can expect services such as talk therapy, also called psychotherapy. The psychologist will work with you to analyze changes in your behavior and uncover the roots of your anxiety. If, for example, your anxiety stems from a previous illness, you may find this particular form of treatment extremely helpful. Based on the severity of your symptoms, the psychologist may refer you to a licensed psychiatrist for medication and further assistance.

Psychiatric Nurse Practitioners and Physician Assistants

If you need treatment for a wide range of mental health conditions, you can receive primary mental health care from psychiatric nurse practitioners and physician assistants. These have the qualifications to diagnose, administer treatments, and even write prescriptions for patients suffering from mental health disorders.

Psychiatrist

If your primary care physician recommended seeing a psychiatrist, you can receive psychotherapy and pharmacological remedies. Psychiatrists are medical doctors who have completed additional training to diagnose and treat mental health conditions. You can rest assured knowing you are in the best hands in the field.

When to See a Doctor

Several people with anxiety symptoms have trouble getting the time right when it comes to seeing the doctor. They often want to avoid looking or sounding petty when they meet their doctor and the doctor confirms that their symptoms are just typical and will clear away in no time. While it may sound embarrassing and make you feel as though you made a big deal out of something petty, it is better to know for sure than keep wondering. If you visit your doctor and they tell you everything is fine, you just go back home and water your beautiful flowers or finish up some projects you had stopped working on due to the symptoms invading your thoughts. What if you ignore your symptoms when they do need attention, only to take action when they become severe? That would be bad for you and your recovery process, so a few guidelines on when to see a doctor are useful for your journey toward fighting anxiety. The following situations may be a sign that you should pick up your phone and make that appointment!

Some people stop and ask themselves if they should seek professional help. Sometimes they even end up disregarding it because, for example, their friend who was in a similar situation didn't seek therapy. This is about you. It is about your sanity, not your friend's. Avoiding options such as therapy is usually due to fear of being judged, but you should keep in mind that seeking assistance isn't a sign of weakness but rather an essential step towards healing. It may be time for you to consult a healthcare professional for advice regarding your anxiety if:

- Your performance at work has deteriorated.

If your anxiety has compromised your ability to work effectively, you may find yourself making costly mistakes at work because your thoughts would be distracting you now and then. It is crucial to seek professional assistance to manage your stress and regain control of your performance.

- You are constantly down and irritable.

We all have those bad days that can make us sad all night long. It is normal to react that way to something disturbing, such as at school or work. Various events can cause one's mood to turn gloomy suddenly, but if that becomes the order of your day, it could be an indication that your anxiety is worsening and you require professional help.

- Your output in school has reduced.

Individuals who suffer from psychological and emotional issues often have trouble paying attention at school. Anxiety problems can make it challenging to concentrate and that causes them to make several mistakes. If your concentration levels have drastically decreased and you suspect it could be due to your anxiety, it is a signal that you have to seek professional intervention.

- You are struggling in your relationships.

Anxiety and contribute to interpersonal conflicts. If you notice that relationships have become strained due to your symptoms it may be time to seek professional help. The symptoms can prevent you from opening up to friends and family and cause you to appear distant or uninterested in relationships. Professional assistance can help salvage relationships.

Preparing to See a Doctor

It is essential to be well-prepared to get the most out of your appointment with the physician. Take a few moments before your appointment with the doctor to think over what you need to tell them and what questions you want to ask them. Writing everything down to avoid leaving out some important questions. Writing things down can also help to avoid panicking when you get there. Having everything in order before you visit your doctor is also important because it helps save time for both you and your healthcare provider. Remember that physicians are busy, especially during crises like this pandemic, but they make time to ensure you are the best version of yourself all the time!

To help your doctor come up with the most accurate diagnosis, you can do the following few things in advance.

- List all your symptoms and indicate how long you have had them.

- Note the circumstances under which your symptoms occur, their impact on your life, as well as situations that lessen the symptoms.

- Share significant life experiences that cause stress, such as any traumas from your past and ongoing ones.

- Jot down all your mental and physical health conditions and all the supplements and medications you take.

- Write down any other substances you consume. These are substances such as alcohol, coffee, tobacco, and drugs that are not part of your treatment regimen, including any other substances you may be taking.

You may also have several questions for your doctor, but if you have not yet listed them somewhere, you might forget them when you go for your appointment, so you also have to jot them down. If you ask a lot of questions for clarity, which is a good thing, you may want to list your questions starting with the most important ones because on busy days you might not have the time to discuss all the questions. Below are some questions you might want to ask your healthcare provider.

- Is my anxiety due to a different health condition?

- What treatment options do I have?

- What are the side effects of the recommended medications?

- Is there anything I can do to prevent or ease the side effects?

- How long after starting treatment will I feel better or notice gradual changes?

Your doctor will also have some questions for you, and you can find some of the questions they may ask you below.

- What symptoms are you experiencing, and when did they start?

- Do you experience your symptoms all the time or at specific times?

- Do you have any physical or mental medical conditions?

- Are you taking any medications at the moment?

- Do you smoke, drink alcohol, use drugs, or consume caffeinated beverages? If so, how frequently, and in what quantity?

- Do you live on your own or with other people? If you live with others, how do you relate to them, and how stressful is your living condition?

- Are you in a relationship, and if so, are you having any difficulties?

- How does your anxiety impact your work, school, or business, and are any of those areas creating pressure?

- Do you have any history of trauma?

Always answer your doctor's questions as truthfully as possible to avoid misdiagnosis. Once your doctor has enough information, they will guide you through what you need to do next.

Therapy

One major problem that hinders most individuals from getting the most out of their therapy sessions is the misconception that once they begin therapy, they will instantly recover. Treatment requires you to work hands-on with your therapist, contribute, and speak up. In some cases, you might even feel worse before you start to notice any changes. Unfortunately, that is the point at which some people quit therapy, saying that it wasn't helping them but only making their situation worse.

You may find that therapy requires you to re-live painful memories and make difficult decisions to move on and leave your past behind. That is usually the part that challenges many individuals and causes them to leave their sessions feeling bad about themselves. However, that is also a tiny issue as long as you cooperate with your therapist as openly as possible. Remember that helping you discover and make peace with your emotions is their specialty, so you are in good hands.

When you finally decide to get help for your anxiety, it's usually because you have tried everything you can to get rid of it on your own but have been unsuccessful. In therapy sessions, you will delve deeper into the causes of your anxiety and the factors that contribute to its manifestations. Your anxiety levels may temporarily increase as a result of this.

It's important to remember that psychotherapy is not a quick remedy. The process is different for every single person who goes through it. Your particular kind of anxiety and the severity of your symptoms will determine every aspect of your treatment, including the type of therapy you require, the skills you will acquire, and the length of time you will spend participating in treatment. You need to have the mindset that although going through the process may not always seem pleasant, it will be well worth it in the end.

Types of Therapy for Anxiety

The goal of all types of therapy is to help you understand why you feel the way you do, what pushes your anxiety buttons, and how you may alter the way you react to your triggers in the future. Some forms of therapy even show you strategies you can practice to help reframe negative thought patterns and turn unwanted behaviors around.

Because of the wide variety of anxiety disorders, treatment must be individualized to address each person's unique set of symptoms and individual diagnosis. Your unique symptoms and diagnosis will determine how often and for how long you should make appointments to see your therapist.

Psychiatrists, therapists, and other experts who work in the field of mental health make use of numerous approaches to treat symptoms of anxiety. Your diagnosis and the severity of your symptoms are also important considerations in selecting an appropriate treatment course.

Cognitive Behavioral Therapy

You may have come across this before, but let us discuss how you can make it work for you. Cognitive behavioral therapy, CBT, is a therapy for various mental health problems that also works well in regulating symptoms of anxiety in several people. It revolves around the idea that your thoughts, not your external environment, are the primary factor in determining how you feel and behave. Therefore, the purpose of CBT is to help you see and comprehend the patterns of your negative thinking and behavior, and then to assist you in replacing those trends with more realistic beliefs, effective behaviors, and healthy coping mechanisms.

During this time, your therapist will serve as a coach, guiding you through the process and giving you useful methods. For instance, if you engage in a lot of *black-and-white thinking* in which you believe that things are either completely negative or completely positive. You would rather replace those thoughts with the more realistic notion that there are a variety of gradations of gray that exist in between.

The tactics that your therapist will put in play require some practice. In CBT your therapist will show you how to manage fear and panic through coping skills. Once you learn how to apply this, you will eventually understand the triggers that cause your anxiety.

Exposure Therapy

One of the most frequent forms of psychotherapy that therapists use to treat several anxiety disorders, is exposure therapy. The idea behind exposure therapy is that the best approach to overcoming a phobia is to confront it head-on. This is the central tenet of the practice.

During exposure treatment, your therapist will gradually bring you into contact with things or circumstances that cause you to feel anxious. The method known as *systematic desensitization* is frequently used to do this, and it consists of the following:

- To assist you in managing your anxiety, your therapist will provide you with steps on how to practice relaxation. Examples of relaxation training include exercises such as guided visualization and deep breathing.

- Write a list of things that bring on anxious feelings for you, and then arrange triggers from least to most severe.

- Exposure involves you progressively making your way through the things or situations on your list that cause you anxiety, employing relaxation techniques as needed.

Your treating provider can choose from a few different approaches to introduce you to the stimuli that cause you to experience anxiety. Here are some of the most frequent:

- Imaginal exposure is a form of exposure in which your healthcare provider gives instructions to vividly visualize an object or circumstance that makes you anxious.

- In vivo exposure is a strategy involving putting yourself in situations or confronting objects that make you anxious in a real environment. For example, with this form of exposure, if you suffer from social anxiety, your therapist may have you deliver a presentation in front of a group of people.

- Exposure to virtual reality: In certain circumstances, where in vivo exposure isn't feasible, one alternative is to use virtual reality. Through technology, virtual reality therapy combines aspects of in vivo and imaginal exposure.

Psychoanalytic Therapy

The aim of psychoanalytic therapy is to find solutions to problems that result from the symptoms of your anxiety. Your psychoanalyst helps you through this by analyzing your thoughts, fears, and desires to gain a deeper understanding of how you perceive yourself and to lessen the amount of anxiety you feel. It can take years of consistent work until your mental healthcare provider uncovers patterns in your way of thinking, but you will see notable progress and it is worth it once you are through. Although they are often used interchangeably, psychoanalytic and psychodynamic treatments are different.

Psychoanalysis is a subcategory of psychodynamic therapy, one of the most intensive forms of treatment.

Interpersonal Therapy

The primary areas of attention in interpersonal therapy, IPT, are interpersonal relationships and social roles. During IPT, you and your therapist will work together to determine if you have any interpersonal issues, such as unresolved sorrow, disputes with family or friends, changes in work or social roles, and problems relating to others. This is yet another form of therapy that can make you feel a little more miserable before you notice progress, but that response is a sign of progress. It is normal to sometimes feel sad during this therapy because it can unravel some events from your past that you had packed away to avoid constant pain. You will then discover constructive ways to express your feelings and methods to increase your ability to communicate with others.

Remember:

You sign up for a long-term commitment when you choose or agree to therapy. If you keep at it, you will reap the fruits of your effort, but if you go easy on it, you will gradually stumble and fall. Below are some suggestions to help you get the most out of your therapy sessions.

- Avoid acting as if you're okay because if your challenges don't show on your face and your therapist misses them, you're not going anywhere else but home with the same problems.

- Draw motivation from the prize. Remind yourself why this is important, and fix your eyes on the success that awaits you.

- Strive to surround yourself with the right people, the ones who care and will stop at nothing to encourage you.

- Avoid situations and people who drain your energy or drag you backward.

- Avoid missing appointments. You must be present to learn coping strategies.

When you put these few things into practice and work consistently with your therapist, your future in overcoming anxiety through therapy becomes brighter.

Chapter 5:

Treatment Options

Available treatments for anxiety include pharmacological and non-pharmacological options. The choice of treatment that you and your healthcare provider choose heavily depends on clinical presentation and the severity of your symptoms. For mild symptoms, you may only need non-pharmacological options such as therapy. The treatment of choice for moderate to severe symptoms is a combination of non-pharmacological options and pharmacological agents. This chapter will focus on available pharmacological treatment options, indications, cautions, side effects, and possible complications that can arise with each treatment option.

Selective Serotonin Reuptake Inhibitors

The first line of treatment for anxiety disorders is a group of drugs called selective serotonin reuptake inhibitors, SSRIs. They were first introduced on the market in the late 1980s after approval by the Food and Drug Agency, FDA. This group of drugs was first used for the treatment of depression but has also shown to be effective in treating anxiety (Furukawa et al., 2016).

As their name suggests, selective serotonin reuptake inhibitors work by preventing serotonin reuptake in the brain at the level of neurons. To better understand them, we need to look at the hormone *serotonin*, also known as the feel-good hormone. Serotonin regulates various processes such as mood, sexual desires, sleep cycle, mental focus, and of course, anxiety.

When we have low serotonin levels, we experience a disturbance in the areas of our life processes that need it. Aggression, poor impulse control, sleeplessness, impatience, and low self-esteem can all be symptoms of low serotonin levels. The impact of low serotonin levels doesn't end there; it extends to eating disorders, obsessive-compulsive disorders, depression, and anxiety disorders. Because anxiety is related to low serotonin levels, SSRIs block the reabsorption of serotonin in the neurons, allowing an adequate amount of serotonin to be available, thereby increasing the levels in the brain. This will improve your mood and reduce your anxiety.

Selective serotonin reuptake inhibitors are available in various formulations, including pills, capsules, and liquid suspensions. If your doctor prescribes these, they usually instruct you to take them once daily, either in the morning or at night. Depending on your doctor's prescribed dosage, you can see gradual results within four to six weeks. Examples of SSRIs include Paroxetine (Paxil), escitalopram (Lexapro), sertraline (Zoloft), fluoxetine (Prozac), fluvoxamine (Luvox), and citalopram (Citalopram).

Selective serotonin reuptake inhibitors can have side effects that you should look out for. Remember that the side-effects others encounter may not be what you experience because each body is different. Some side effects of SSRIs may include, but are not limited to:

- loss of libido
- fatigue
- dry mouth
- weight gain
- restlessness
- nausea
- vomiting
- diarrhea

Serotonin-Norepinephrine Reuptake Inhibitors

Other antidepressant medications that are effective in the treatment are serotonin-norepinephrine reuptake inhibitors, SNRIs. Although SNRIs are most commonly prescribed for the treatment of depression, the FDA authorized the usage of some of them for the management of anxiety disorders.

SNRIs enhance the levels of active neurotransmitters in the brain by inhibiting the reuptake (also known as reabsorption) of serotonin and norepinephrine back into the nerve cells that released them. Both neurotransmitters are linked to different structures and activities in the brain, and they have slightly diverse effects on various processes, such as how one feels and how much energy they provide.

Some examples of SNRIs include:

- Venlafaxine (Effexor)
- Duloxetine (Cymbalta)
- Desvenlafaxine (Pristiq)
- Levomilnacipran (Fetzima)

SNRIs have a few health risks, but here are some side effects they can have:

- headache
- nausea
- profuse sweating
- elevated levels of blood pressure
- dizziness
- anxiety
- having trouble getting to sleep
- dizziness

Benzodiazepines

Another class of drugs used to treat anxiety is called benzodiazepines. This group of drugs has been used to treat disorders such as seizures, anxiety, sleep disorders, and alcohol withdrawal. In addition to that, they are used for general anesthesia.

Benzodiazepines work on receptors of neurons called *gamma-aminobutyric acid*, GABA. Gamma-aminobutyric acid is an inhibitory receptor that blocks specific messages or neurotransmitters in the brain, causing relaxing effects. Benzodiazepines bind on GABA A, a subunit of GABA structure. The binding results in the release of negatively charged chloride, which makes the neurons in the brain at the site of synapses less responsive to other excitatory neurotransmitters. The overall result is you feeling calmer and more relaxed.

Some examples of benzodiazepines include:

Alprazolam (Xanax)

Diazepam (Valium)

Lorazepam (Ativan)

Chlordiazepoxide (Librium)

Unlike SSRIs, benzodiazepines act fast once in your body's system. Their onset of action can range from minutes to an hour if you take them orally and just a few minutes if you get an injection.

Benzodiazepines can have side effects that include:
- respiratory depression
- confusion
- headache
- syncope
- nausea
- diarrhea
- tremors
- drowsiness
- hallucinations
- euphoria

Excess quantities of the excitatory neurotransmitter glutamate can cause *excitotoxicity* which causes damage and even death to brain cells. Excitotoxicity is too much excitement of brain neurons that causes toxicity. Symptoms may also appear after a progressive dosage reduction, but they are usually milder and can last for months after you withdraw from benzodiazepine. The most successful method of managing withdrawal is a cautious and progressive withdrawal tailored to the person and, if required, psychological help. The period required to complete withdrawal varies widely, ranging from weeks to several months.

Buspirone

Another group of drugs that is available for use in the treatment of anxiety is *buspirone*, an anxiolytic medication that was initially developed for the treatment of psychosis but could not keep up. It was ineffective in the treatment of psychosis. Unlike other drugs used to treat anxiety, buspirone has no antiseizure, hypnotic or muscle-relaxant effects, hence the name anxioselective. Its mechanism of action is complex and challenging to pinpoint, but the common understanding is that it is a serotonin agonist. That means it stimulates serotonin receptors on the nerves. It also has some impact on dopamine, and that helps in balancing one's mood. It can take up to four weeks to see the effects of the drugs after initiation of the treatment course.

When an individual does not respond to selective serotonin reuptake inhibitors or cannot endure their side effects, their healthcare providers can use buspirone as a treatment option. Buspirone can also be taken with or without SSRIs. Healthcare providers also use buspirone as a supplement to help minimize the sexual adverse effects of SSRIs. Unlike benzodiazepines, buspirone does not act on GABA receptors and therefore poses a decreased risk of physical dependence or withdrawal.

Some side effects of buspirone can include:
- headaches
- dizziness

- drowsiness
- nausea
- vomiting
- diarrhea
- nervousness
- unexplained excitement
- confusion
- depression

Sometimes individuals overdose on medicines such as buspirone to stimulate themselves. In high doses, this substance does not produce euphoria but rather dizziness, nausea, and body intoxication. High buspirone dose can happen on purpose, as in the case of purposeful drug misuse, or unintentionally, as in the instance of someone mixing prescriptions or drinking alcohol while the drug is still in their system. You should seek immediate medical care if you notice symptoms of buspirone overdose.

Beta Blockers

Another group of drugs that healthcare professionals use to treat anxiety symptoms is beta blockers. Doctors also use these drugs to treat conditions such as hypertension, heart failure, and hyperthyroidism. Even though various studies have proved how effective beta blockers are, the FDA has not yet approved its use in treating anxiety. Beta blockers are used off-label to treat anxiety.

Beta blockers work on *beta adrenergic receptors* which play a vital part in the fight or flight mode. When stimulated, these receptors produce the hormone adrenaline or noradrenaline. Adrenaline causes your heart to beat fast, heart muscles to contract harder, your breathing rate to increase, and it also raises your level of alertness. The same stimulation process is how anxiety comes about, so beta blockers work by preventing that from happening.

There are three known types of beta receptors:

- beta 1 receptors that are mainly found on the heart and kidneys

- beta 2 receptors that are found on smooth muscles such as gastrointestinal system, lungs and bladder

- beta 3 receptors that are found on fat muscles

Beta blockers work by binding on to these receptors and blocking the adrenergic effects that you experience when you have anxiety. They have two different groups, namely: the particular type and the non-selective type. The non-selective type works on all beta receptors. They are generalized, so they can work on the heart, lungs, bladder, and gastrointestinal system. An example of this type of beta blockers is propranolol. The selective beta blockers work on a specific beta receptor amongst those mentioned above three. An example is an atenolol, which exclusively works on beta one receptors. Both drugs, atenolol and propranolol, are used in the treatment of anxiety.

According to a current observational data set, atenolol may be well-tolerated and valuable in the treatment of anxiety disorders. These findings also imply that atenolol, rather than propranolol, may be the beta-blocker that doctors prefer to prescribe for anxiety problems.

Some side effects of beta-blockers can include:

- nausea
- diarrhea
- bronchospasm
- dyspnea
- cold extremities
- bradycardia
- hypotension
- heart failure
- heart block
- fatigue
- dizziness
- alopecia
- abnormal vision
- hallucinations

- insomnia
- nightmares
- sexual dysfunction
- erectile dysfunction

Hydroxyzine

Hydroxyzine is a first-generation antihistamine developed in the 1950s and works to treat allergic reactions such as itching and nausea. Healthcare providers also use it to treat sleeping difficulties and anxiety itself. Hydroxyzine is the only antihistamine the FDA has approved to treat anxiety. It binds to histamine receptors that are stimulated when there is an allergic reaction. The block that it creates reduces reactions and also causes sleepiness. The magical effects of hydroxyzine kick in with a notable impact within 30 minutes, and it plunges into full effect within two hours. While it is excellent that it works rapidly, however, many of its potential effects on you will manifest themselves quickly as well.

Some side effects of hydroxyzine may include:

- sedation
- difficulty concentrating
- nausea

- vomiting
- dry mouth
- dry eyes

Points to Remember

It is essential to keep in mind that different people will react differently, so while some people experience little to no side effects, some will have the opposite experience. Be sure to notify your health care provider if you experience side effects to medications. Your health care provider will inform you if you need to change or continue with the medication.

Note that you shouldn't use the information provided in this chapter as a substitute for direct medical advice. Always consult a medical professional for reliable advice and refrain from taking medication without your doctor's consent. Do not take medicines without a prescription and do not share drugs. Even if your friend or family member has similar symptoms as yours, taking the pills they were given by their doctor isn't ideal because what applies to them might not work for you. Also, taking someone else's prescription can be unsafe and even fatal.

Chapter 6:

Moving On

We all have lost someone or something during the COVID-19 pandemic. It is the way of life, but have you accepted it? Although we react differently to loss and deal with emotions in our unique ways, we all have in common that life must go on. You and I have to move on! Accepting loss is complex, and it is a process, a very demanding one. Don't let anyone tell you otherwise. Read that again: Moving on is hard but possible. With the suitable approaches, you can get through your hardships and losses and live again. This chapter takes you through healing from the effects of the pandemic, a significant step toward accepting the damage that the outbreak left.

Dealing with Loss

You may have lost your job, marriage, a loved one or anything of grave value during the COVID-19 pandemic. Whatever or whoever it is, the loss still hurts when realization surges through your blood, leading you through the notorious grief process. You get all kinds of questions and answer some on your own, but others lurk in the back of your mind, poking you out of your mental comfort every once in a while. Grief can worsen your anxiety, so it is essential to master a few survival skills, especially now that loss seems to be in the air. Accepting defeat is one of the stages of grieving during the pandemic, but you do not just wake up at the doorstep to acceptance; there are steps that take you there.

Stages of Grief

In 1969, Elisabeth Kübler-Ross, a Swiss-American psychiatrist who studied near-death situations, described a hypothetical model to explain stages of grief. Known as the Kübler-Ross model, her representation has five phases (Corr, 2018). It is essential to understand that the steps do not necessarily follow each other. One stage may last longer in one individual than the other, and sometimes the grieving individual may go through the same phases repeatedly before they reach the level of acceptance. Even so, understanding the steps is an excellent starting point for you to move on despite experiencing anxiety during this time of hardship.

Anger

Remember, we have established that grief during the pandemic is associated with many other emotions than sadness. If you lost your loved one, you might be angry at the way life can just end without giving prior notice, or you might wonder why it happened to you. No one puts a tag on you to declare that bad thing should happen, so although you may ponder over why the loss occurred, most of those negative occurrences are natural. You may show frustration, irritability, and impatience when going through the anger phase during the pandemic. In worse scenarios, the anger may come with deeper emotions such as resentment and rage. You may feel your loss was unfair, no one understands your challenges, or you may also think of the loss as someone's fault and stir toward revenge.

Anger makes you prone to short-temper and emotional instability. You will have trouble tolerating genuine mistakes and may become aggressive verbally, physically, or both ways. Mismanagement of anger amidst the coronavirus disease outbreak can also cause you to rely on substances such as drugs and alcohol, but misuse of those will only cause you more harm. You can try the following strategies to cope with anger during a time of grief.

- Let yourself feel the impact. Find a safe space to digest your emotions and reflect on the losses you encountered as a result of the COVID-19 pandemic. You can reflect on your difficult experiences in a quiet place alone or with a friend.

- Dissect any underlying feelings to address other sources of your anger that may or may not be directly related to the impact of the pandemic. Doing that will help you realize what you have to work on before your feelings turn into aggression or other negative emotions.

- Give yourself room to feel angry because when you repress your emotions, they tend to surface in worse forms, such as internalized self-hatred.

- Try expressing your thoughts and emotions through activities such as poetry or painting if you are not ready to put your feelings into words.

- Consider other people's perspectives to better comprehend their side of the story. If you are grieving over a marriage you lost during the pandemic or other issues involving two or more parties, trying to understand the other person's point of view can give you closure.

The cycle between thoughts and results can keep you going in circles if you do not change it. Thoughts cause feelings, which cause behaviors, which cause thoughts again. Disrupt one element of your cycles, adjust your perspective and rewire your behavior to fight anger more effectively during the COVID-19 pandemic.

Denial

Your brain has a defense mechanism to protect you from difficult emotions. In the denial phase of grief, the protective mechanism makes you act as though the loss didn't occur, while giving you more time to get used to the changes that come with the loss. For example, if you lost your job due to the outbreak or some unforeseen causes, you may have to adjust to being home all day while you determine your next step. If you lost someone with whom you shared a house, you can expect a few changes in your daily schedule, the plates at the dinner table, and even the atmosphere in the house.

As you start processing the impact of the loss you experienced during the COVID-19 pandemic, you may also feel other emotions such as guilt, sadness, rage, or anxiety. You may blame yourself for some of the events leading up to your loss, you may feel sad about your loved one not being with you anymore, or you may be enraged about your favorite pet getting injured. During this stage, the loss feels unbelievable, it doesn't make sense.

When going through the denial stage of grief, you may experience some of the following:

- confusion and disorientation
- numbness
- increased sleep time
- procrastination of issues related to the loss
- forgetfulness regarding issues related to the loss
- inability to digest feelings and emotions

During denial, you may have a constant longing to contact the person you lost during the pandemic. Some people who lost marriages during the pandemic thought of ways to reconcile with their partners despite knowing their situation could not be helped. Here are a few steps you can use to cut off chains if you find yourself trapped in denial:

- Remember that healing is a process and will require some time. The most effective way to deal with denial during a time of grief is to give it time.

- Consider the future because although it will be hard to live your life as normal after suffering a major loss, you can only move forward.

- Do not be afraid to envision your life past the loss, because as soon as you feel prepared, you can start taking baby steps toward your future.

- You can also tap into journaling. Keeping journals is helpful for some individuals, but you will have to use the journal with caution to avoid trapping yourself in the past or dwelling too much on the pain the COVID-19 pandemic caused you.

Bargaining

It is common to have such desperation while dealing with loss that you would be willing to try virtually anything to lessen the suffering. When a loved one passes away, we may think of ways to reduce the grief we are currently experiencing or the pain we anticipate from loss. We can try to negotiate in a variety of ways.

You would probably offer to do anything to bring your loved one back if you lost them during the COVID-19 outbreak. As an alternative, you might consider whether you could have avoided the loss by being a better person or acting differently. Even if you have lost something significant, such as a career, business, friendship, physical ability, or a sense of control or independence, you could still have these ideas.

If you feel this way, you are not alone. During the grieving process, bargaining is a common and normal response to loss. The bargaining stage is about negotiations, a variety of them. Some sound guilty, some fearful, and others desperate beyond measure. You may promise to be more loving if you feel or think your loss resulted from you not showing enough affection. People at loss during the pandemic may bargain in the present by trying to reach an agreement with themselves, or with a higher power for those who have religious beliefs. They may negotiate with the understanding that if they act in a certain manner, they might feel better or the situation might improve. In several other cases, individuals at loss may bargain over the past by reflecting on all the things they did and didn't do, things they wish to modify if they could go back in time to avoid the loss.

When we begin to bargain, we frequently address a higher power or something more powerful than ourselves that could be able to affect a different result with our requests. We become acutely conscious of our humanity when we acknowledge that there is nothing we can do to affect change or a better outcome.

We may respond in defiance to this sensation of helplessness by bargaining, which offers us a sense of control over something that feels so out of our control. We tend to dwell on our mistakes or regrets when we bargain. When we reflect on our encounters with the person we lost, we can notice all the times we felt distant from them or might have harmed them.

It is common to think back on situations where we may have spoken things we didn't mean and wish we could change how we behaved. We frequently assume that if events transpired differently, we would not currently be in such a difficult emotional situation.

Try some of these hacks to cope with bargaining when you are grieving during or even after the pandemic:

- Accept bargaining as a means to hang on to hope despite the impact the pandemic has had on you. It reduces over time as you start to accept reality, but before then, you need hope to keep going.

- Your discomfort will probably get easier to handle over time, and you could find it easier to accept events beyond your control. However, even years after a death, mourning for some people continues to be incredibly difficult. It's essential to discuss your symptoms with a doctor or mental health expert if you're not feeling any better.

- Instead of dwelling on thoughts about how much pain the COVID-19 pandemic caused you, try to distract yourself from them as you work your way toward acceptance.

- Write down your feelings, ideas, and thoughts. You can never go wrong with expressing yourself on paper, especially during this time of crisis. You can think about your sentiments, bargains, and wishes while you explore more about your genuine feelings and motivations instead of drowning yourself in them.

- Adjust your views and expectations, especially when dealing with loss that is beyond your control, such as a loved one. Once you realize that you can't change what already happened, you become better equipped to move forward despite the pain the pandemic caused you.

- Accept help. Understand that there is no shame in accepting help when people who care offer it to you during this time of pain and suffering. You can even ask for assistance yourself if you find yourself wrapped up in a cycle of blame and guilt, or if your grief is worsening your anxiety during or after the COVID-19 pandemic.

Depression

There comes the point in the grieving process when denial fades and you gradually consider the reality of your situation. During the COVID-19 pandemic, depression is a phase during which you face the truth of your situation and know that negotiating is no longer an option. Your grief over the impact of the pandemic becomes more intense, and the emotional haze starts to lift as your terror decreases. This is the point at which you realize the magnitude of your loss and its effect on your anxiety. As the depression intensifies during this difficult time, you may withdraw from social engagements, become less friendly, and even censor your struggle during this difficult time so as to not scare those around you.

Although depression is a natural stage of grief, dealing with it can be hard, scary, and lonely during the COVID-19 pandemic. You may experience sadness and depression if you are mourning the death of something or someone you lost because of the pandemic. You may feel like giving up on things you used to care about before the coronavirus disease hit us hard. It may be tough for you to get out of bed and go about your day the way you did before the pandemic struck because you feel overburdened by the pain it caused you.

You are not alone if you feel this way. At any stage of the grieving process, a person may feel depressed or exhibit other symptoms of depression. Their feelings and symptoms may also vary in length, regularity, and intensity. Understanding the traits and symptoms of the depression stage of grieving during the pandemic is useful because it can help you spot some of the situations you can go through as you try to recover from the impact of the pandemic.

During the depression stage of grief, you may feel empty and sad about the unfortunate events that occurred in your life because of the COVID-19 pandemic. Life can feel overwhelming to the extent that you withdraw from others and avoid any offers for help because of the fear that your grief may overwhelm them during this period when they probably have their own bruises to recover from as well.

Symptoms of depression during the pandemic can worsen if you withdraw from others, and that makes it difficult for you to cope with your anxiety. It is important to accept help from friends, family, coworkers, spiritual leaders, and other people you think can be of assistance during this time of hardship. Refrain from suppressing your feelings and focus on accepting all your emotions because there is no right or wrong feeling. We all feel what we feel, and that is just it. Avoid self-criticism because it exacerbates depressive symptoms. Create a particular routine to digest the loss and pain that the pandemic caused you. Reach out for support if you need assistance.

Acceptance

In the end, all pieces fall in place. When you reach the acceptance stage, it's not that you stop feeling the grief of loss, but you are no longer fighting against the truth of your circumstances or the pain that the COVID-19 pandemic caused you.

Peace and Happiness

Many people can testify that their anxiety increases when they think about disturbing incidents and problems that COVID-19 already caused them, as well as ponder over the probability of it creating new problems for them in the future. If you feel the same, you may have noticed that the same thoughts keep running through your mind in a never-ending loop, which only worsens your level of anxiety during this difficult time. This pattern of thinking not only contributes nothing to the solution of the problems at hand, but it also has the potential to obstruct you from recovering from the damage that the pandemic caused in your life.

Someone may have advised you in the past to clear your mind in order to let go of tension, but this strategy isn't really about letting go of all of the thoughts and worries that hover in your mind. Instead, working on positivity and inner peace is about learning how you can become more focused as well as how to control your thoughts without pressuring your mind. This strategy will leave you better equipped to take action and address most of the negative thought patterns that contribute to your anxiety. Establishing this calm state of mind also requires you to be happy, but that raises yet another question about how you can achieve happiness. This question is at the core of many of the objectives that we all strive to achieve. Happiness is typically the experience of joyous feelings and a sense of fulfillment in one's life. It is something you can learn by experimenting with various strategies. You can move on from the pain that the coronavirus pandemic caused you by changing the way you think and by making the necessary changes to your daily life.

Finding strategies to make yourself happy despite the effects of the coronavirus pandemic begins by taking baby steps that help you progress toward larger goals over the long term. Spend some time considering the aspects of your life that will contribute to your sense of contentment and positivity, and think about the steps you can take to move closer to achieving some of the objectives you have set for yourself. Just keep in mind that there is no set location, time, or weather for happiness. It is the process of designing a life that provides you with happiness, meaning, and a genuine sense of accomplishment. It's not necessary to wait in order to feel better and become more content; there are actions that you can take now to achieve this goal.

Bear in mind, though, that the concept of happiness can mean a variety of things to different people.

You can bring more joy and contentment into your life by first analyzing the current circumstances of your life, determining how happy you already are, and then selecting a course of action to pursue closure and the strength to heal from all the pain the coronavirus outbreak caused you.

You can regain your happiness even if you thought you'd lost it, and that's one of the best things about establishing peace and seeking happiness amidst the coronavirus pandemic. It is something that can be accomplished regardless of whether you choose to look backward for happiness or forward into uncharted territory in search of a fresh source of joy. We can't control the unpredictability of life, and we are not guaranteed happiness every single day, but we can work toward having more happy days than sad ones. When we establish peace with the losses we suffered during the pandemic, we gain the strength to look back and enjoy the excellent times that we had despite its impact on our lives.

Another common misperception about establishing peace and happiness during the pandemic lies in the effort it requires. Several people tend to think that moving past the pain and inconveniences it caused them is impossible, but sometimes all you have to do is participate in activities that you take pleasure in.

You don't have to go far to find peace and happiness during and after the coronavirus pandemic because they are right there, waiting for you to get up on your feet and claim them. Take the required actions to get you back to the place that brings you joy. You will be relieved that you made that decision once you remove any obstacles that may be preventing you from achieving your perfect environment. Figure out what exactly you are looking forward to and get up to start working on your happiness right this second!

Find Your Joy

The first thing you need to do to make yourself happy despite the impact of the coronavirus disease in your life is to determine what brings you the most pleasure and fulfillment. This entails evaluating the things in your life that genuinely make you happy, rather than trying to follow other people's expectations of joy during this difficult time.

Several individuals often get caught up chasing imaginations such as the ideal home, romantic partner, or family, but after all this pain and suffering, do you have the time to wander in search of ideals? Besides, what if you never find that? Embarking on a journey to find ideal partners, jobs and friends can worsen your anxiety because then you will keep wandering and wondering. Even after all that work and you think you have found your ideal partner or friend, you may feel disappointed again after some time when what you once thought to be ideal turns out not to be all that great.

On other occasions, you may set your mind so squarely on a particular objective that you believe can bring you happiness during the coronavirus pandemic, leaving no room in your schedules for other aspects of your life that will actually bring you long-lasting peace and joy during this difficult time.

Several people have taken steps to move on from the pain and inconveniences that the COVID-19 pandemic caused them. The time and effort that it requires is worth it when you finally find the strength to move on and continue with your life despite the impact of the coronavirus disease. If others can move on and forge a happy future despite the pandemic, you can too!

Conclusion

Marked here, is the beginning of your new adventure, a journey toward overcoming anxiety during the pandemic and lasting after the pandemic. In this book, we covered anxiety from what it is, its symptoms, as well as the different forms in which anxiety disorders present. We also briefly analyzed the impact of the COVID-19 pandemic on anxiety, and provided various strategies to fight anxiety. You can also implement some simple lifestyle changes at home, to the pharmaceutical drugs that are available for treating symptoms of anxiety. Now you can go out there in confidence, knowing you have enough weapons to fight your anxiety and eventually toss those nagging thoughts off your mind for good!

If you found this book helpful and enjoyable, feel free to share it with your family and friends so that it benefits them as well.

References

A quote by Vicki Harrison. (n.d.). *Goodreads.* https://www.goodreads.com/quotes/543175-grief-is-like-the-ocean-it-comes-on-waves-ebbing

Achour, M., Souici, D., Bensaid, B., Binti Ahmad Zaki, N., & Alnahari, A. A. A. (2021). Coping with anxiety during the COVID-19 Pandemic: A case study of academics in the Muslim world. *Journal of Religion and Health, 60*(6), 4579–4599. https://doi.org/10.1007/s10943-021-01422-3

Bhanot, D., Singh, T., Verma, S. K., & Sharad, S. (2021). Stigma and discrimination during COVID-19 pandemic. *Frontiers in Public Health, 8.* https://doi.org/10.3389/fpubh.2020.577018

Chaturvedi, K., Kumar Vishwakarma, D., & Singh, N. (2020). COVID-19 and its impact on education, social life and mental health of students: A survey. *Children and Youth Services Review, 121*(105866), 105866. https://doi.org/10.1016/j.childyouth.2020.105866

Cherry, K. (2022, February 21). *Are you in a healthy relationship?* Verywell Mind.

https://www.verywellmind.com/all-about-healthy-relationship-4774802

Corr, C. A. (2018). Elisabeth Kübler-Ross and the "Five Stages" Model in a Sampling of Recent American Textbooks. *OMEGA - Journal of Death and Dying, 82*(2), 003022281880976. https://doi.org/10.1177/0030222818809766

Cuncic, A. (n.d.). *What is radical acceptance?* Verywell Mind. Retrieved June 2022, from https://www.verywellmind.com/what-is-radical-acceptance-5120614#toc-coping-statements-for-radical-acceptance

Excelsior, G. (2014). *The light of reason: The delight of the awakened state*. BalboaPress.

Ferguson, J. M. (2001). SSRI antidepressant medications: Adverse effects and tolerability. *Primary Care Companion to the Journal of Clinical Psychiatry, 3*(1), 22–27. https://www.ncbi.nlm.nih.gov/pmc/articles/PMC181155/

Fornaro, M., Anastasia, A., Valchera, A., Carano, A., Orsolini, L., Vellante, F., Rapini, G., Olivieri, L., Di Natale, S., Perna, G., Martinotti, G., Di Giannantonio, M., & De Berardis, D. (2019). The FDA "black box" warning on antidepressant suicide risk in young adults: More harm than benefits?. *Frontiers in Psychiatry, 10.* https://doi.org/10.3389/fpsyt.2019.00294

Frankl, V. E. (2013). *Man's Search For Meaning: The classic tribute to hope from the Holocaust.* Ebury Digital.

Fuller, K. (n.d.). *How to sleep better.* Verywell Mind. https://www.verywellmind.com/how-to-get-better-sleep-5094084

Furukawa, T. A., Salanti, G., Atkinson, L. Z., Leucht, S., Ruhe, H. G., Turner, E. H., Chaimani, A., Ogawa, Y., Takeshima, N., Hayasaka, Y., Imai, H., Shinohara, K., Suganuma, A., Watanabe, N., Stockton, S., Geddes, J. R., & Cipriani, A. (2016). Comparative efficacy and acceptability of first-generation and second-generation antidepressants in the acute treatment of major depression: Protocol for a network meta-analysis. *BMJ Open, 6*(7), e010919. https://doi.org/10.1136/bmjopen-2015-010919

Gupta, S. (2021, December 27). *How to build trust in a relationship.* Verywell Mind. https://www.verywellmind.com/how-to-build-trust-in-a-relationship-5207611

Gupta, S. (2022a, May 24). *What to know about the anger stage of grief.* Verywell Mind. https://www.verywellmind.com/the-anger-stage-of-grief-characteristics-and-coping-5295703

Gupta, S. (2022b, May 26). *What to know about the denial stage of grief*. Verywell Mind. https://www.verywellmind.com/the-denial-stage-of-grief-characteristics-and-coping-5272456

Gupta, S. (n.d.). *What to know about the bargaining stage of grief*. Verywell Mind. Retrieved June 2022, from https://www.verywellmind.com/the-bargaining-stage-of-grief-characteristics-and-coping-5272529

Holland, K. (2018, May). *What triggers anxiety? 11 causes that may surprise you*. Healthline. https://www.healthline.com/health/anxiety/anxiety-triggers

Jodi Clarke. (2021, February 12). *What to know about the five stages of grief*. Verywell Mind. https://www.verywellmind.com/five-stages-of-grief-4175361

Klevebrant, L., & Frick, A. (2022). Effects of caffeine on anxiety and panic attacks in patients with panic disorder: A systematic review and meta-analysis. *General Hospital Psychiatry, 74*, 22–31. https://doi.org/10.1016/j.genhosppsych.2021.11.005

Lee, K. (n.d.). *How to nurture your parent-child bond*. Verywell Family. https://www.verywellfamily.com/habits-that-will-strengthen-your-parent-child-bond-620063

Leonard, J. (2018, July 18). *Symptoms, signs, and side effects of anxiety*. Medical News Today. https://www.medicalnewstoday.com/articles/322510

Long, E., Patterson, S., Maxwell, K., Blake, C., Pérez, R. B., Lewis, R., McCann, M., Riddell, J., Skivington, K., Wilson-Lowe, R., & Mitchell, K. R. (2021). COVID-19 pandemic and its impact on social relationships and health. *J Epidemiol Community Health, 76*(2). https://doi.org/10.1136/jech-2021-216690

Morin, A. (2020, July 13). *7 ways to find more meaning and purpose in your life*. Verywell Mind. https://www.verywellmind.com/tips-for-finding-your-purpose-in-life-4164689

Muskin, P. R. (2021). *What are anxiety disorders?* American Psychiatry Association. https://psychiatry.org/patients-families/anxiety-disorders/what-are-anxiety-disorders

National Institute of Mental Health. (2019). *Anxiety disorders*. Nih.gov; National Institute of Mental Health. https://www.nimh.nih.gov/health/topics/anxiety-disorders

Nelson, T., Kagan, N., Critchlow, C., Hillard, A., & Hsu, A. (2020). The danger of misinformation in the COVID-19 crisis. *Missouri Medicine, 117*(6), 510–512.

https://www.ncbi.nlm.nih.gov/pmc/articles/PMC7721433/

NHS. (2019, November 6). *5 steps to mental wellbeing*. Nhs.uk. https://www.nhs.uk/mental-health/self-help/guides-tools-and-activities/five-steps-to-mental-wellbeing/

OECD. (2021). *The impact of COVID-19 on employment and jobs - OECD*. OECD. https://www.oecd.org/employment/covid-19.htm

Saladino, V., Algeri, D., & Auriemma, V. (2020). The psychological and social impact of Covid-19: New perspectives of well-being. *Frontiers in Psychology, 11*(577684). https://doi.org/10.3389/fpsyg.2020.577684

Satre, D. D., Iturralde, E., Ghadiali, M., Young-Wolff, K. C., Campbell, C. I., Leibowitz, A. S., & Sterling, S. A. (2020). Treatment for anxiety and substance use disorders during the COVID-19 pandemic: Challenges and strategies. *Journal of Addiction Medicine*, 14(6), e293–e296. https://doi.org/10.1097/adm.0000000000000755

Scott, E. (2020, August 3). *5 self-care practices for every area of your life*. Verywell Mind. https://www.verywellmind.com/self-care-strategies-overall-stress-reduction-3144729

Scott, E. (2021, July 29). *17 highly effective stress relievers*. Verywell Mind. https://www.verywellmind.com/tips-to-reduce-stress-3145195

The Healthline Editorial Team. (2014, August 18). *Doctors who treat anxiety: What to say and ask*. Healthline. https://www.healthline.com/health/anxiety-doctors#:~:text=A%20psychiatrist%20is%20a%20medical

Ullman, M. (2019). *8 reasons why you're not sleeping well and what to do about it*. Verywell Mind. https://www.verywellmind.com/reasons-for-not-sleeping-well-and-how-to-fix-350760

World Health Organization. (2022, March). *COVID-19 pandemic triggers 25% increase in prevalence of anxiety and depression worldwide*. WHO. https://www.who.int/news/item/02-03-2022-covid-19-pandemic-triggers-25-increase-in-prevalence-of-anxiety-and-depression-worldwide

Made in the USA
Columbia, SC
23 November 2022